BOOKS BY MARTIN BUBER

MARTIN BUBER

I and Thou

Translated by Ronald Gregor Smith

SCRIBNER CLASSICS

New York   London   Toronto   Sydney   Singapore

SCRIBNER
1230 Avenue of the Americas
New York, NY 10020

First Scribner Classics edition 2000

SCRIBNER and design are trademarks of
Macmillan Library Reference USA, Inc., used under
license by Simon & Schuster, the publisher of this work.

DESIGNED BY ERICH HOBBING

Manufactured in the United States of America

3 5 7 9 10 8 6 4 2

The Library of Congress has cataloged the
Scribner/Collier edition as follows:
Buber, Martin, 1878–1965.
I and thou.
(A Scribner classic)
Translation of : Ich und du.
Reprint. Originally published: New York : Scribner's, 1958.
1. Life. 2. Relationism. 3. God—Knowableness.
I. Title. II. Series: Scribner classic.
B3213.B831213   1986
181.06   86-6885

ISBN 0-7432-0133-7

TRANSLATOR'S PREFACE
TO THE SECOND EDITION

IT IS NOW ALMOST THIRTY-FIVE YEARS since *Ich und Du* first appeared in Germany, and over twenty years since the first English edition. Since that time Martin Buber's work has become widely known in a great variety of fields. In the present book, as well as in later works which illustrate or add to it, he has something specific to say to many kinds of specialists: to educators, to doctors, to politicians, to sociologists, to biblical critics, even to poets, and certainly to theologians and philosophers.

In my original introduction I tried to express my awareness of a kind of revolutionary simplicity in the content of *I and Thou.* Many of the early readers shared that sense, so that some were even inclined to say that *I and Thou,* after all, was only saying what a candid reader might find in the primitive message of the New Testament, especially in the teaching of Jesus. There is this amount of truth in this view, that Buber, deeply immersed as he is in the concretion, the historical and dramatic forms of thinking characteristic of his Hebrew tradition, has been able, both in *I and Thou* and in many of his later writings, in some measure to recover and to express the unique force at work in the Christian tradition as well. The two traditions, the Jewish and the Christian, are indeed separated by a specific confession about certain historical events; but they are looking all the time at the same events. It is the point on the way, not the way itself, which is different. Moreover, the expectation characteristic of Buber's writing is not dissolved in the Christian tradition, but is embodied in a faith which, though markedly eschatological, still has hope as one of its chief elements. In *I and Thou* the two traditions interact and illuminate one another in a remarkable and moving way.

But in my early attempt to introduce English-speaking readers to what Buber has to say I was in the main content to point simply to the effect Buber was already having upon theological thought—and, of course, at that time chiefly in Germany. The many printings of the English edition which have appeared since 1937 mention the work of Karl Heim, Friedrich Gogarten and Eberhard Grisebach. It is now possible to add the names of Paul Tillich and Karl Barth, though with these two writers the connexions are intricate, and certainly do not allow talk of any mere "influence" of Buber's thought in a simple way. Buber's own *Nachwort* to the volume *Schriften über das dialogische Prinzip* (Heidelberg, 1954), has a highly interesting comment on Barth's position as expressed in his *Kirchliche Dogmatik,* in the second part of the "Doctrine of Creation." To this might be added the remarkable recent essay by Barth, *Die Menschlichkeit Gottes* ("Theologische Studien," Nr. 48, 1956). But a discussion of this connexion would take us too far. Nor need we mention here more than a few names of those in the Anglo-Saxon world who since then have explicitly acknowledged Buber's influence: J. H. Oldham, M. Chaning-Pearce, John Baillie, H. H. Farmer, Reinhold Niebuhr, Sir Herbert Read. The list could be extended, and no doubt it could range into other fields, especially those of psychotherapy and education. Leslie H. Farber, for instance, the Chairman of the Faculty, The Washington School of Psychiatry, has recently paid a remarkable tribute (in *Psychiatry*, May 1957) to Buber's work in its relation to the work of psychiatrists and social scientists.

The serious question, however, is not how far writers in various fields of interest have found Buber's thought congenial and illuminating, how far they have really entered into his main concern, and how far they have simply made a certain use of his distinctions and categories: these matters, though interesting both in themselves and as material for a study of the shifting thought-forms of our time, must be left aside in this note. The serious question is how each reader is to approach Buber's work, especially the present book, and what he is to expect of it.

This is certainly not a normal question in the approach to most writers; but it is necessary here. In my original introduction I spoke of Buber as a poet, and even as a mystic of a certain kind. I am still inclined to retain, with reservations, the description of "poet"; but the description of "mystic" is on the whole one that leads to too great a danger of misunderstanding, and should be rejected. Of course there are many kinds of mystics, as there are many kinds of poets. But in the end, it seems, there is no word to describe the remarkable combination in Buber's writing of concrete imagery and situation with a sense of overtones, and at the same time with a kind of directness which lays a special claim upon the reader. It is this last element, the element of claim, calling for a specific response, which might make it possible to use of Buber's work a word which has become fashionable in recent years—namely, "existentialist"; but this word, too, has many different associations. Certainly, in Buber's work the connexion with the "father" of existentialism, Søren Kierkegaard, is clear and unmistakable; and the content of Buber's experience, with its wide range—through nature and history, and including the "eternal Thou," the Absolute Person—can offer a corrective to much truncated and emaciated existentialism in our time.

But however one may seek to define these elements, a reader of *I and Thou* must come with the question rising up in himself which is *the* question for Buber: how may I understand my experience of a relation with God? To speak of this relation in such a way that it is neither subdued by any intolerance clinging to a dogmatic form, nor left as a mere ripple of sensation upon an otherwise meaningless existence; to speak of it in terms which do not merely identify it with concepts or with feelings, but do justice to its inner nature—this is Buber's chief concern. He speaks, therefore, however qualified his language, of a direct or immediate relation with God. I do not intend to enlarge upon the questions raised by such a description: clearly it is the terminology which lends most justification to the description of Buber as a "mystic." How to join this understanding of the chief element in man's life as direct relation to God with an understanding of concrete human experience is a difficulty which Buber himself faces anew in the Postscript he has written for this edition. What in any case is clear is that Buber does speak out of what he himself regards as a relation with God which is basic to true humanity: a relation largely unrecognised today, yet one which is essential for the recovery of true humanity in all spheres. This relation he presents in *I and Thou* with a variety and subtlety and richness of experience which are at the same time able to convey the sense of that relation as a presence and a demand upon the reader.

If this is the main concern throughout the book—and indeed, as Buber himself says in the Postscript, through almost all his writings—then the now familiar categories of *I–Thou* and *I–It* which are unfolded here must be seen as taking a secondary place. They are pointers to the human situation, in its intricate interweaving of the personal and the impersonal, of the world to be "used" and the world to be "met." But the very intricacy of that situation makes it very difficult, if not impossible, to use these distinctions as a kind of open sesame to the whole world of our experience. It is certainly necessary that I should warn the reader against a too facile assumption of these distinctions as involving clear-cut divisions between two worlds in which man may move. There is *one* world, which is twofold; but this twofoldness cannot be allocated to (let us say) on the one hand the scientist with a world of *It* and (let us say) on the other hand the poet with a world of *Thou*. Rather, this twofoldness runs through the whole world, through each person, each human activity. To recognise this is to recognise the need for reserve, for concreteness, for what Buber elsewhere calls "the hallowing of the every-day." Any situation may become the vehicle of the "eternal Thou." Human existence today, in its particular peril, cannot be rescued by any shibboleth, but only by the kind of sober re-appraisal which may be found in the pages of this book.

In particular, it is worth drawing the reader's attention to Buber's explanations given in the new Postscript. Especially in his reiteration of what he means by the personal, and by God as Person, he has enriched his position against a possible objection from the side of an ontological assertion about God's being. While maintaining the category of the personal as strictly attributable to God, he has to some extent obviated the criticism that God and man might be considered as being equal partners in a conversation. It is, I suspect, against such a position, derived by others, not by Buber himself, from Buber's dialogical personalism, that Paul Tillich is speaking, when he writes (in his *Systematic Theology*, I, 127) that "If it [revelation] is brought down to the level of a conversation between two beings, it is blasphemous and ridiculous." For Buber himself God's transcendence, his absolute otherness, is so thoroughly involved in his whole understanding of the relation between God and man, that it is difficult to select one point rather than another in his exposition of this. The otherness which runs through man's whole relation to his world points to this transcendence, at the same time as the transcendence is drawn into the whole world. I do not mean that Buber himself would use such a term as transcendence, but that the reality to which this term points is fully present in the thought of *I and Thou*.

From my original introduction I now repeat the last two paragraphs. The inadequacy of a translation to do more than hint at the power of the original is specially noticeable with a poetical work of this kind. Footnotes might have helped to explain a word or two, or indicate nuances of the German which the English has lost; but, though the word might have been explained, the impact of the argument would have been dissipated rather than strengthened. The text stands therefore without any commentary. To the reader who finds the meaning obscure at a first reading we may only say that *I and Thou* is indeed a poem. Hence it must be read more than once, and its total effect allowed to work on the mind; the obscurities of one part (so far as they are real obscurities, and not the effect, as they must often be, of poor translation) will then be illumined by the brightness of another part. For the argument is not as it were horizontal, but spiral; it mounts, and gathers within itself the aphoristic and pregnant utterances of the earlier part.

I have to thank many friends and helpers for advice given at various points, in particular Frau Dr. Elisabeth Rotten, of Saanen, Switzerland, who repaired a little of the havoc I wrought at points with the original text, and most of all Dr. Buber himself, whose courteous and encouraging help lightened my task considerably.

Only one or two verbal changes have been made in the text of this edition: I now use "spiritual beings" for "geistige Wesenheiten" on pages 22 and 98, and now translate "Umkehr" by "turning" (which is more in line with biblical usage than the rather obscure "reversal").

R.G.S.
Glasgow University,
November 1957

CONTENTS

So, waiting, I have won from you the end: God's presence in each element.

GOETHE

I and Thou

Part One

To MAN THE WORLD IS TWOFOLD, in accordance with his twofold attitude.

The attitude of man is twofold, in accordance with the twofold nature of the primary words which he speaks.

The primary words are not isolated words, but combined words.

The one primary word is the combination *I–Thou*.

The other primary word is the combination *I–It;* wherein, without a change in the primary word, one of the words *He* and *She* can replace *It*.

Hence the *I* of man is also twofold.

For the *I* of the primary word *I–Thou* is a different *I* from that of the primary word *I–It*.

◆

PRIMARY WORDS DO NOT SIGNIFY THINGS, but they intimate relations.

Primary words do not describe something that might exist independently of them, but being spoken they bring about existence.

Primary words are spoken from the being.

If *Thou* is said, the *I* of the combination *I–Thou* is said along with it.

If *It* is said, the *I* of the combination *I–It* is said along with it.

The primary word *I–Thou* can only be spoken with the whole being.

The primary word *I–It* can never be spoken with the whole being.

◆

THERE IS NO *I* TAKEN IN ITSELF, but only the *I* of the primary word *I–Thou* and the *I* of the primary word *I–It*.

When a man says *I* he refers to one or other of these. The *I* to which he refers is present when he says *I*. Further, when he says *Thou* or *It*, the *I* of one of the two primary words is present.

The existence of *I* and the speaking of *I* are one and the same thing.

When a primary word is spoken the speaker enters the word and takes his stand in it.

◆

THE LIFE OF HUMAN BEINGS is not passed in the sphere of transitive verbs alone. It does not exist in virtue of activities alone which have some *thing* for their object.

I perceive something. I am sensible of something. I imagine something. I will something. I feel something. I think something. The life of human beings does not consist of all this and the like alone.

This and the like together establish the realm of *It*.

But the realm of *Thou* has a different basis.

When *Thou* is spoken, the speaker has no thing for his object. For where there is a thing there is another thing. Every *It* is bounded by others; *It* exists only through being bounded by others. But when *Thou* is spoken, there is no thing. *Thou* has no bounds.

When *Thou* is spoken, the speaker has no *thing;* he has indeed nothing. But he takes his stand in relation.

◆

IT IS SAID THAT MAN EXPERIENCES HIS WORLD. What does that mean?

Man travels over the surface of things and experiences them. He extracts knowledge about their constitution from them: he wins an experience from them. He experiences what belongs to the things.

But the world is not presented to man by experiences alone. These present him only with a world composed of *It* and *He* and *She* and *It* again.

I experience something.—If we add "inner" to "outer" experiences, nothing in the situation is changed. We are merely following the uneternal division that springs from the lust of the human race to whittle away the secret of death. Inner things or outer things, what are they but things and things!

I experience something.—If we add "secret" to "open" experiences, nothing in the situation is changed. How self-confident is that wisdom which perceives a closed compartment in things, reserved for the initiate and manipulated only with the key. O secrecy without a secret! O accumulation of information! It, always It!

◆

THE MAN WHO EXPERIENCES has not part in the world. For it is "in him" and not between him and the world that the experience arises.

The world has no part in the experience. It permits itself to be experienced, but has no concern in the matter. For it does nothing to the experience, and the experience does nothing to it.

◆

AS EXPERIENCE, the world belongs to the primary word *I–It*.

The primary word *I–Thou* establishes the world of relation.

◆

THE SPHERES IN WHICH THE WORLD OF RELATION ARISES are three.

First, our life with nature. There the relation sways in gloom, beneath the level of speech. Creatures live and move over against us, but cannot come to us, and when we address them as *Thou,* our words cling to the threshold of speech.

Second, our life with men. There the relation is open and in the form of speech. We can give and accept the *Thou.*

Third, our life with spiritual beings. There the relation is clouded, yet it discloses itself; it does not use speech, yet begets it. We perceive no *Thou,* but none the less we feel we are addressed and we answer—forming, thinking, acting. We speak the primary word with our being, though we cannot utter *Thou* with our lips.

But with what right do we draw what lies outside speech into relation with the world of the primary word?

In every sphere in its own way, through each process of becoming that is present to us we look out toward the fringe of the eternal *Thou;* in each we are aware of a breath from the eternal *Thou;* in each *Thou* we address the eternal *Thou.*

✦

I CONSIDER A TREE.

I can look on it as a picture: stiff column in a shock of light, or splash of green shot with the delicate blue and silver of the background.

I can perceive it as movement: flowing veins on clinging, pressing pith, suck of the roots, breathing of the leaves, ceaseless commerce with earth and air—and the obscure growth itself.

I can classify it in a species and study it as a type in its structure and mode of life.

I can subdue its actual presence and form so sternly that I recognise it only as an expression of law—of the laws in accordance with which a constant opposition of forces is continually adjusted, or of those in accordance with which the component substances mingle and separate.

I can dissipate it and perpetuate it in number, in pure numerical relation.

In all this the tree remains my object, occupies space and time, and has its nature and constitution.

It can, however, also come about, if I have both will and grace, that in considering the tree I become bound up in relation to it. The tree is now no longer *It*. I have been seized by the power of exclusiveness.

To effect this it is not necessary for me to give up any of the ways in which I consider the tree. There is nothing from which I would have to turn my eyes away in order to see, and no knowledge that I would have to forget. Rather is everything, picture and movement, species and type, law and number, indivisibly united in this event.

Everything belonging to the tree is in this: its form and structure, its colours and chemical composition, its intercourse with the elements and with the stars, are all present in a single whole.

The tree is no impression, no play of my imagination, no value depending on my mood; but it is bodied over against me and has to do with me, as I with it—only in a different way.

Let no attempt be made to sap the strength from the meaning of the relation: relation is mutual.

The tree will have a consciousness, then, similar to our own? Of that I have no experience. But do you wish, through seeming to succeed in it with yourself, once again to disintegrate that which cannot be disintegrated? I encounter no soul or dryad of the tree, but the tree itself.

◆

IF I FACE A HUMAN BEING AS MY *Thou*, and say the primary word *I–Thou* to him, he is not a thing among things, and does not consist of things.

Thus human being is not *He* or *She*, bounded from every other *He* and *She*, a specific point in space and time within the net of the world; nor is he a nature able to be experienced and described, a loose bundle of named qualities. But with no neighbour, and whole in himself, he is *Thou* and fills the heavens. This does not mean that nothing exists except himself. But all else lives in *his* light.

Just as the melody is not made up of notes nor the verse of words nor the statue of lines, but they must be tugged and dragged till their unity has been scattered into these many pieces, so with the man to whom I say *Thou*. I can take out from him the colour of his hair, or of his speech, or of his goodness. I must continually do this. But each time I do it he ceases to be *Thou*.

And just as prayer is not in time but time in prayer, sacrifice not in space but space in sacrifice, and to reverse the relation is to abolish the reality, so with the man to whom I say *Thou*. I do not meet with him at some time and place or other. I can set him in a particular time and place; I must continually do it: but I set only a *He* or a *She*, that is an *It*, no longer my *Thou*.

So long as the heaven of *Thou* is spread out over me the winds of causality cower at my heels, and the whirlpool of fate stays its course.

I do not experience the man to whom I say *Thou*. But I take my stand in relation to him, in the sanctity of the primary word. Only when I step out of it do I experience him once more. In the act of experience *Thou* is far away.

Even if the man to whom I say *Thou* is not aware of it in the midst of his experience, yet relation may exist. For *Thou* is more that *It* realises. No deception penetrates here; here is the cradle of the Real Life.

◆

THIS IS THE ETERNAL SOURCE OF ART: a man is faced by a form which desires to be made through him into a work. This form is no offspring of his soul, but is an appearance which steps up to it and demands of it the effective power. The man is concerned with an act of his being. If he carries it through, if he speaks the primary word out of his being to the form which appears, then the effective power streams out, and the work arises.

The act includes a sacrifice and a risk. This is the sacrifice: the endless possibility that is offered up on the altar of the form. For everything which just this moment in play ran through the perspective must be obliterated; nothing of that may penetrate the work. The exclusiveness of what is facing it demands that it be so. This is the risk: the primary word can only be spoken with the whole being. He who gives himself to it may withhold nothing of himself. The work does not suffer me, as do the tree and the man, to turn aside and relax in the world of *It;* but it commands. If I do not serve it aright it is broken, or it breaks me.

I can neither experience nor describe the form which meets me, but only body it forth. And yet I behold it, splendid in the radiance of what confronts me, clearer than all the clearness of the world which is experienced. I do not behold it as a thing among the "inner" things nor as an image of my "fancy," but as that which exists in the present. If test is made of its objectivity the form is certainly not "there." Yet what is actually so much present as it is? And the relation in which I stand to it is real, for it affects me, as I affect it.

To produce is to draw forth, to invent is to find, to shape is to discover. In bodying forth I disclose. I lead the form across—into the world of *It.* The work produced is a thing among things, able to be experienced and described as a sum of qualities. But from time to time it can face the receptive beholder in its whole embodied form.

◆

—WHAT, THEN, DO WE EXPERIENCE OF *Thou*?
  —Just nothing. For we do not experience it.
  —What, then, do we know of *Thou*?
  —Just everything For we know nothing isolated about it any more.

Plato's concept of absolute forms

◆

THE *Thou* MEETS ME THROUGH GRACE—it is not found by seeking. But my speaking of the primary word to it is an act of my being, is indeed *the* act of my being.

The *Thou* meets me. But I step into direct relation with it. Hence the relation means being chosen and choosing, suffering and action in one; just as any action of the whole being, which means the suspension of all partial actions and consequently of all sensations of actions grounded only in their particular limitation, is bound to resemble suffering.

The primary word *I–Thou* can be spoken only with the whole being. Concentration and fusion into the whole being can never take place through my agency, nor can it ever take place without me. I become through my relation to the *Thou;* as I become *I*, I say *Thou*.

All real living is meeting.

◆

THE RELATION TO THE *Thou* IS DIRECT. No system of ideas, no foreknowledge, and no fancy intervene between *I* and *Thou*. The memory itself is transformed, as it plunges out of its isolation into the unity of the whole. No aim, no lust, and no anticipation intervene between *I* and *Thou*. Desire itself is transformed as it plunges out of its dream into the appearance. Every means is an obstacle. Only when every means has collapsed does the meeting come about.

◆

IN FACE OF THE DIRECTNESS of the relation everything indirect becomes irrelevant. It is also irrelevant if my *Thou* is already the *It* for other *I*'s ("an object of general experience"), or can become so through the very accomplishment of this act of my being. For the real, though certainly swaying and swinging, boundary runs neither between experience and non-experience, nor between what is given and what is not given, nor yet between the world of being and the world of value; but cutting indifferently across all these provinces it lies between *Thou* and *It,* between the present and the object.

◆

THE PRESENT, and by that is meant not the point which indicates from time to time in our thought merely the conclusion of "finished" time, the mere appearance of a termination which is fixed and held, but the real, filled present, exists only in so far as actual presentness, meeting, and relation exist. The present arises only in virtue of the fact that the *Thou* becomes present.

The *I* of the primary word *I–It,* that is, the *I* faced by no *Thou,* but surrounded by a multitude of "contents," has no present, only the past. Put in another way, in so far as man rests satisfied with the things that he experiences and uses, he lives in the past, and his moment has no present content. He has nothing but objects. But objects subsist in time that has been.

The present is not fugitive and transient, but continually present and enduring. The object is not duration, but cessation, suspension, a breaking off and cutting clear and hardening, absence of relation and of present being.

True beings are lived in the present, the life of objects is in the past.

◆

APPEAL TO A "WORLD OF IDEAS" as a third factor above this opposition will not do away with its essential twofold nature. For I speak of nothing else but the real man, of you and of me, of our life and of our world—not of an *I,* or a state of being, in itself alone. The real boundary for the actual man cuts right across the world of ideas as well.

To be sure, many a man who is satisfied with the experience and use of the world of things has raised over or about himself a structure of ideas, in which he finds refuge and repose from the oncome of nothingness. On the threshold he lays aside his inauspicious everyday dress, wraps himself in pure linen, and regales himself with the spectacle of primal being, or of necessary being; but his life has no part in it. To proclaim his ways may even fill him with well-being.

But the mankind of mere *It* that is imagined, postulated, and propagated by such a man has nothing in common with a living mankind where *Thou* may truly be spoken. The noblest fiction is a fetish, the loftiest fictitious sentiment is depraved. Ideas are no more enthroned above our heads than resident in them; they wander amongst us and accost us. The man who leaves the primary word unspoken is to be pitied; but the man who addresses instead these ideas with an abstraction or a password, as if it were their name, is contemptible.

◆

IN ONE OF THE THREE EXAMPLES it is obvious that the direct relation includes an effect on what confronts me. In art the act of the being determines the situation in which the form becomes the work. Through the meeting that which confronts me is fulfilled, and enters the world of things, there to be endlessly active, endlessly to become *It*, but also endlessly to become *Thou* again, inspiring and blessing. It is "embodied"; its body emerges from the flow of the spaceless, timeless present on the shore of existence.

The significance of the effect is not so obvious in the relation with the *Thou* spoken to men. The act of the being which provides directness in this case is usually understood wrongly as being one of feeling. Feelings accompany the metaphysical and metapsychical fact of love, but they do not constitute it. The accompanying feelings can be of greatly differing kinds. The feeling of Jesus for the demoniac differs from his feeling for the beloved disciple; but the love is the one love. Feelings are "entertained": love comes to pass. Feelings dwell in man; but man dwells

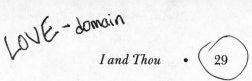

in his love. That is no metaphor, but the actual truth. Love does not cling to the *I* in such a way as to have the *Thou* only for its "content," its object; but love is *between I* and *Thou.* The man who does not know this, with his very being know this, does not know love; even though he ascribes to it the feelings he lives through, experiences, enjoys, and expresses. Love ranges in its effect through the whole world. In the eyes of him who takes his stand in love, and gazes out of it, men are cut free from their entanglement in bustling activity. Good people and evil, wise and foolish, beautiful and ugly, become successively real to him; that is, set free they step forth in their singleness, and confront him as *Thou.* In a wonderful way, from time to time, exclusiveness arises—and so he can be effective, helping, healing, educating, raising up, saving. Love is responsibility of an *I* for a *Thou.* In this lies the likeness—impossible in any feeling whatsoever—of all who love, from the smallest to the greatest and from the blessedly protected man, whose life is rounded in that of a loved being, to him who is all his life nailed to the cross of the world, and who ventures to bring himself to the dreadful point—to love *all men.*

Let the significance of the effect in the third example, that of the creature and our contemplation of it, remain sunk in mystery. Believe in the simple magic of life, in service in the universe, and the meaning of that waiting, that alertness, that "craning of the neck" in creatures will dawn upon you. Every word would falsify; but look! round about you beings live their life, and to whatever point you turn you come upon being.

◆

RELATION IS MUTUAL. My *Thou* affects me, as I affect it. We are moulded by our pupils and built up by our works. The "bad" man, lightly touched by the holy primary word, becomes one who reveals. How we are educated by children and by animals! We live our lives inscrutably included within the streaming mutual life of the universe.

◆

—YOU SPEAK OF LOVE as though it were the only relation between men. But properly speaking, can you take it even only as an example, since there is such a thing as hate?

—So long as love is "blind," that is, so long as it does not see a *whole* being, it is not truly under the sway of the primary word of relation. Hate is by nature blind. Only a part of a being can be hated. He who sees a whole being and is compelled to reject it is no longer in the kingdom of hate, but is in that of human restriction of the power to say *Thou.* He finds himself unable to say the primary word to the other human being confronting him. This word consistently involves an affirmation of the being addressed. He is therefore compelled to reject either the other or himself. At this barrier the entering on a relation recognises its relativity, and only simultaneously with this will the barrier be raised.

Yet the man who straightforwardly hates is nearer to relation than the man without hate and love.

◆

BUT THIS IS THE EXALTED MELANCHOLY OF OUR FATE, that every *Thou* in our world must become an *It.* It does not matter how exclusively present the *Thou* was in the direct relation. As soon as the relation has been worked out or has been permeated with a means, the *Thou* becomes an object among objects—perhaps the chief, but still one of them, fixed in its size and its limits. In the work of art realisation in one sense means loss of reality in another. Genuine contemplation is over in a short time; now the life in nature, that first unlocked itself to me in the mystery of mutual action, can again be described, taken to pieces, and classified—the meeting-point of manifold systems of laws. And love itself cannot persist in direct relation. It endures, but in interchange of actual and potential being. The human being who was even now single and unconditioned, not something lying to hand, only present, not able to be experienced, only able to be fulfilled, has now become again a *He* or a *She,* a sum of qualities, a given quantity with a certain shape. Now I may take out from him again the colour of his hair or of his speech or of his goodness. But so long as I can do this he is no more my *Thou* and cannot yet be my *Thou* again.

Every *Thou* in the world is by its nature fated to become a thing, or continually to re-enter into the condition of things. In objective speech it would be said that every thing in the world, either before or after becoming a thing, is able to appear to an *I* as its *Thou.* But objective speech snatches only at a fringe of real life.

The *It* is the eternal chrysalis, the *Thou* the eternal butterfly— except that situations do not always follow one another in clear succession, but often there is a happening profoundly twofold, confusedly entangled.

◆

IN THE BEGINNING IS RELATION.

Consider the speech of "primitive" peoples, that is, of those that have a meagre stock of objects, and whose life is built up within a narrow circle of acts highly charged with presentness. The nuclei of this speech, words in the form of sentences and original pre-grammatical structures (which later, splitting asunder, give rise to the many various kinds of words), mostly indicate the wholeness of a relation. We say "far away"; the Zulu has for that a word which means, in our sentence form, "There where someone cries out: 'O mother, I am lost.' " The Fuegian soars above our analytic wisdom with a seven-syllabled word whose precise meaning is, "They stare at one another, each waiting for the other to volunteer to do what both wish, but are not able to do." In this total situation the persons, as expressed both in nouns and pronouns, are embedded, still only in relief and without finished independence. The chief concern is not with these products of analysis and reflection but with the true original unity, the lived relation.

We greet the man we meet, wishing him well or assuring him of our devotion or commending him to God. But how indirect these worn-out formulas are! What do we discern even dimly in "Hail!" of the original conferring of power? Compare these with the ever fresh Kaffir greeting, with its direct bodily relation, "I see you!" or with its ridiculous and sublime American variant, "Smell me!"

It may be supposed that characterisations and ideas, but also representations of persons and things, have been taken out from representations of incidents and situations that are specifically relational. The elementary impressions and emotional stirrings that waken the spirit of the "natural man" proceed from incidents—experience of a being confronting him—and from situations—life with a being confronting him—that are relational in character. He is not disquieted by the moon that he sees every night, till it comes bodily to him, sleeping or waking, draws near and charms him with silent movements, or fascinates him with the evil or sweetness of its touch. He does not retain from this the visual representation, say, of the wandering orb of light, or of a demonic being that somehow belongs to it, but at first he has in him only the dynamic, stirring image of the moon's effect, streaming through his body. Out of this the image of the moon personally achieving the effect only gradually emerges. Only now, that is to say, does the memory of the unknown that is nightly taken into his being begin to kindle and take shape as the doer and bringer of the effect. Thus it makes possible the transformation of the unknown into an object, a *He* or a *She* out of a *Thou* that could not originally be experienced, but simply suffered.

This initial and long-continuing relational character of every essential phenomenon makes it also easier to understand a certain spiritual element of primitive life that is much discussed and observed, but not yet properly grasped, in present-day study. I mean that mysterious power the idea of which has been traced, through many variations, in the form of the beliefs or in the knowledge (both being still one) of many nature peoples. Known as

Mana or Orenda, it opens a way to the Brahman in its primal meaning, and further to the Dynamis and Charis of the Magical Papyri and of the Apostolic Epistles. It has been characterised as a supersensuous or supernatural power—descriptions which depend on our categories and do not correspond to those of the primitive man. The limits of his world are set by his bodily experience, to which visits from the dead, say, quite "naturally" belong. To accept what has no sensuous qualities at all as actually existing must strike him as absurd. The appearances to which he ascribes the "mystical power" are all elementary incidents that are relational in character, that is, all incidents that disturb him by stirring his body and leaving behind in him a stirring image. The moon and the dead, visiting him by night with pain or pleasure, have that power. But so, too, have the burning sun and the howling beast and the chief whose glance constrains him and the sorcerer whose singing loads him with power for the hunt. Mana is simply the effective force, that which has made the person of the moon, up there in the heavens, into a blood-stirring *Thou*. The memory of it left its track when the image of the object was separated out from the total stirring image; although it itself, indeed, never appears other than in the doer and bringer of an effect. It is that with which man himself, if he possesses it—perhaps in a wonderful stone— can be effective in this way. The "world-image" of primitive man is magical not because human magical power is set in the midst of it but because this human power is only a particular variety of the general magic power from which all effective action is derived. Causality in his world-image is no unbroken sequence but an ever new flashing forth of power and moving out towards its production; it is a volcanic movement without continuity. Mana is a primitive abstraction, probably more primitive than, say, number, but not any more supernatural than it. The memory, as it is being trained ranges the grand relational events, the elemental emotional shocks. The most important for the instinct of preservation and the most noteworthy for the instinct to understand—that is, "that which effects," stands out most forcibly of all, and becomes independent. The less important, the non-communal, the changing *Thou* of experiences, retires and remains isolated in the memory, and is gradually transformed into an object and very slowly drawn into groups and classes. As third in the arrangement, terrible when thus separated, at times more ghostly than the dead and the moon, but always more and more irrefutably clear, there arises up the other, "unchanging" partner, "I."

Consciousness of the "I" is not connected with the primitive sway of the instinct for self-preservation any more than with that of the other instincts. It is not the "I" that wishes to propagate iself, but the body, that knows as yet of no "I." It is not the "I" but the body that wishes to make things, a tool or a toy, that wishes to be a "creator." Further, a *cognosco ergo sum,* in however naïve a form and however childlike a conception of an experiencing subject, cannot be found in the primitive function of knowledge. The "I" emerges as a single element out of the primal experiences, out of the vital primal words *I–affecting–Thou* and *Thou–affecting–I,* only after they have been split asunder and the participle has been given eminence as an object.

◆

THE FUNDAMENTAL DIFFERENCE between the two primary words comes to light in the spiritual history of primitive man. Already in the original relational event he speaks the primary word *I–Thou* in a natural way that precedes what may be termed visualisation of forms—that is, before he has recognised himself as *I.* The primary word *I–It,* on the other hand, is made possible at all only by means of this recognition—by means, that is, of the separation of the *I.*

The first primary word can be resolved, certainly, into *I* and *Thou,* but it did not arise from their being set together; by its nature it precedes *I.* The second word arose from the setting together of *I* and *It:* by nature it comes after *I.*

In the primitive relational event, in virtue of its exclusiveness, the *I* is included. While, that is to say, there are in it, in accordance with its being, only the two partners, the man and that which confronts him, in their full actuality, and while the world becomes in it a dual system, the man, without yet perceiving the *I* itself, is already aware of that cosmic pathos of the *I*.

On the other hand the *I* is not yet included in the natural, actual event which is to pass over into the primary word *I–It*, into the experience with its relation to *I*. This actual event is the separation of the human body, as the bearer of its perceptions, from the world round about it. The body comes to know and to differentiate itself in its peculiarities; the differentiation, however, remains one of pure juxtaposition, and hence cannot have the character of the state in which *I* is implied.

But when the *I* of the relation has stepped forth and taken on separate existence, it also moves, strangely tenuous and reduced to merely functional activity, into the natural, actual event of the separation of the body from the world round about it, and awakens there the state in which *I* is properly active. Only now can the conscious act of the *I* take place. This act is the first form of the primary word *I–It*, of the experience in its relation to *I*. The *I* which stepped forth declares itself to be the bearer, and the world round about to be the object, of the perceptions. Of course, this happens in a "primitive" form and not in the form of a "theory of knowledge." But whenever the sentence "I see the tree" is so uttered that it no longer tells of a relation between the man—*I*—and the tree—*Thou*—, but establishes the perception of the tree as object by the human consciousness, the barrier between subject and object has been set up. The primary word *I–It*, the word of separation, has been spoken.

◆

—THAT MELANCHOLY OF OUR FATE, then, arose in earliest history?
—Indeed, yes—in so far as the conscious life of man arose in earli-

est history. But conscious life means the return of cosmic being as human becoming. Spirit appears in time as a product—even as a by-product of nature, yet it is in spirit that nature is timelessly enveloped.

The opposition of the two primary words has many names at different times and in different worlds; but in its nameless truth it is inherent in creation.

body
(mind
prototype
archetype

◆

BUT YOU BELIEVE then in the existence of a paradise in the earliest days of mankind?

—Even if it was a hell—and certainly that time to which I can go back in historical thought was full of fury and anguish and torment and cruelty—at any rate it was not unreal.

The relational experiences of man in earliest days were certainly not tame and pleasant. But rather force exercised on being that is really lived than shadowy solicitude for faceless numbers! From the former a way leads to God, from the latter only one to nothingness.

◆

ONLY BRIEF GLIMPSES into the context in time of the two primary words are given us by primitive man, whose life, even if it could be made fully accessible, can represent only as it were allegorically that of the real early man. We receive fuller knowledge from the child.

Here it becomes crystal clear to us that the spiritual reality of the primary words arises out of a natural reality, that of the primary word *I–Thou* out of natural combination, and that of the primary word *I–It* out of natural separation.

The ante-natal life of the child is one of purely natural combination, bodily interaction and flowing from the one to the other. Its life's horizon, as it comes into being, seems in a unique way to be, and yet again not to be, traced in that of the life that bears it.

For it does not rest only in the womb of the human mother. Yet this connexion has such a cosmic quality that the mythical saying of the Jews, "in the mother's body man knows the universe, in birth he forgets it," reads like the imperfect decipherment of an inscription from earliest times. And it remains indeed in man as a secret image of desire. Not as though his yearning meant a longing to return, as those suppose who see in the spirit—confusing it with their intellect—a parasite of nature, when it is rather (though exposed to diverse illnesses) nature's best flower. But the yearning is for the cosmic connexion, with its true *Thou,* of this life that has burst forth into spirit.

Every child that is coming into being rests, like all life that is coming into being, in the womb of the great mother, the undivided primal world that precedes form. From her, too, we are separated, and enter into personal life, slipping free only in the dark hours to be close to her again; night by night this happens to the healthy man. But this separation does not occur suddenly and catastrophically like the separation from the bodily mother; time is granted to the child to exchange a spiritual connexion, that is, *relation,* for the natural connexion with the world that he gradually loses. He has stepped out of the glowing darkness of chaos into the cool light of creation. But he does not possess it yet; he must first draw it truly out, he must make it into a reality for himself, he must find for himself his own world by seeing and hearing and touching and shaping it. Creation reveals, in meeting, its essential nature as form. It does not spill itself into expectant senses, but rises up to meet the grasping senses. That which will eventually play as an accustomed object around the man who is fully developed, must be wooed and won by the developing man in strenuous action. For no *thing* is a ready-made part of an experience only in the strength, acting and being acted upon, of what is over against men, is anything made accessible. Like primitive man the child lives between sleep and sleep (a great part of his waking hours is also sleep) in the flash and counter-flash of meeting.

The primal nature of the effort to establish relation is already to be seen in the earliest and most confined stage. Before anything isolated can be perceived, timid glances move out into indistinct space, towards something indefinite; and in times when there seems to be no desire for nourishment, hands sketch delicately and dimly in the empty air, apparently aimlessly seeking and reaching out to meet something indefinite. You may, if you wish, call this an animal action, but it is not thereby comprehended. For these very glances will after protracted attempts settle on the red carpet-pattern and not be moved till the soul of the red has opened itself to them; and this very movement of the hands will win from a woolly Teddybear its precise form, apparent to the senses, and become lovingly and unforgettably aware of a complete body. Neither of these acts is experience of an object, but is the correspondence of the child—to be sure only "fanciful"—with what is alive and effective over against him. (This "fancy" does not in the least involve, however, a "giving of life to the universe": it is the instinct to make everything into *Thou*, to give relation to the universe, the instinct which completes out of its own richness the living effective action when a mere copy or symbol of it is given in what is over against him.) Little, disjointed, meaningless sounds still go out persistently into the void. But one day, unforeseen, they will have become conversation—does it matter that it is perhaps with the simmering kettle? It is conversation. Many a movement termed reflex is a firm trowel in the building up of the person in the world. It is simply not the case that the child first perceives an object, then, as it were, puts himself in relation with it. But the effort to establish relation comes first—the hand of the child arched out so that what is over against him may nestle under it; second is the actual relation, a saying of *Thou* without words, in the state preceding the word-form; the thing, like the *I*, is produced late, arising after the original experiences have been split asunder and the connected partners separated. In the beginning is relation—as category of being, readiness, grasping form, mould for the soul; it is the *a priori* of relation, *the inborn Thou.*

The inborn *Thou* is realised in the lived relations with that which meets it. The fact that this *Thou* can be known as what is over against the child, can be taken up in exclusiveness, and finally can be addressed with the primary word, is based on the *a priori* of relation.

In the instinct to make contact (first by touch and then by visual "touch" of another being) the inborn *Thou* is very soon brought to its full powers, so that the instinct ever more clearly turns out to mean mutual relation, "tenderness." But the instinct to "creation," which is established later (that is, the instinct to set up things in a synthetic, or, if that is impossible, in an analytic way—through pulling to pieces or tearing up), is also determined by this inborn *Thou,* so that a "personification" of what is made, and a "conversation," take place. The development of the soul in the child is inextricably bound up with that of the longing for the *Thou,* with the satisfaction and the disappointment of this longing, with the game of his experiments and the tragic seriousness of his perplexity. Genuine understanding of this phenomenon, which is injured by every attempt to lead it back into more confined spheres, can only be promoted if, during its observation and discussion, its cosmic and metacosmic origin is kept in mind. For it reaches out from the undivided primal world which precedes form, out of which the bodily individual who is born into the world, but not yet the personal, actualised being, has fully emerged. For only gradually, by entering into relations, is the latter to develop out of this primal world.

◆

THROUGH THE *Thou* a man becomes *I.* That which confronts him comes and disappears, relational events condense, then are scattered, and in the change consciousness of the unchanging partner, of the *I,* grows clear, and each time stronger. To be sure, it is still seen caught in the web of the relation with the *Thou,* as the increasingly distinguishable feature of that which reaches out to and yet is not the *Thou.* But it continually breaks through with more power, till a time comes when it bursts its bonds, and the *I* confronts itself for a moment, separated as though it were a *Thou;* as quickly to take possession of itself and from then on to enter into relations in consciousness of itself.

Only now can the other primary word be assembled. Hitherto the *Thou* of relation was continually fading away, but it did not thereby become an *It* for some *I,* an object of perception and experience without real connexion—as it will henceforth become. It became rather an *It,* so to speak, for itself, an *It* disregarded at first, yet waiting to rise up in a new relational event. Further, the body maturing into a person was hitherto distinguished, as bearer of its perceptions and executor of its impulses, from the world round about. But this distinction was simply a juxtaposition brought about by its seeing its way in the situation, and not an absolute severance of *I* and its object. But now the separated *I* emerges, transformed. Shrunk from substance and fulness to a functional point, to a subject which experiences and uses, *I* approaches and takes possession of all *It* existing "in and for itself," and forms in conjunction with it the other primary word. The man who has become conscious of *I,* that is, the man who says *I-It,* stands before things, but not over against them in the flow of mutual action. Now with the magnifying glass of peering observation he bends over particulars and objectifies them, or with the field-glass of remote inspection he objectifies them and arranges them as scenery, he isolates them in observation without any feeling of their exclusiveness, or he knits them into a scheme of observation without any feeling of universality. The feeling of exclusiveness he would be able to find only in relation, the feeling of universality only through it. Now for the first time he experiences things as sums of qualities. From each relational experience qualities belonging to the remembered *Thou* had certainly remained sunk in his memory; but now for the first time things are for him actually composed of their qualities. From the simple memory of the relation the man, dreaming or fashioning or thinking, according to his nature, enlarges the nucleus, the substance that showed itself in the *Thou* with power and gathered up in itself all qualities. But now also for the first time he sets things in space and time, in causal connexion, each with its own place and appointed course, its measurability and conditioned nature.

The *Thou* appears, to be sure, in space, but in the exclusive situation of what is over against it, where everything else can be only the background out of which it emerges, not its boundary and measured limit. It appears, too, in time, but in that of the event which is fulfilled in itself: it is not lived as part of a continuous and organised sequence, but is lived in a "duration" whose purely intensive dimension is definable only in terms of itself. It appears, lastly, simultaneously as acting and as being acted upon—not, however, linked to a chain of causes, but, in its relation of mutual action with the *I,* as the beginning and the end of the event. This is part of the basic truth of the human world, that only *It* can be arranged in order. Only when things, from being our *Thou,* become our *It,* can they be co-ordinated. The *Thou* knows no system of co-ordination.

But now that we have come so far, it is necessary to set down the other part of the basic truth, without which this would be a useless fragment—namely, a world that is ordered is not the world-order. There are moments of silent depth in which you look on the world-order fully present. Then in its very flight the note will be heard; but the ordered world is its indistinguishable score. These moments are immortal, and most transitory of all; no content may be secured from them, but their power invades creation and the knowledge of man, beams of their power stream into the ordered world and dissolve it again and again. This happens in the history both of the individual and of the race.

◆

To MAN THE WORLD IS TWOFOLD, in accordance with his twofold attitude.

He perceives what exists round about him—simply things, and beings as things; and what happens round about him—simply events, and actions as events; things consisting of qualities, events of moments; things entered in the graph of place, events in that of time; things and events bounded by other things and events, measured by them, comparable with them: he perceives an ordered and detached world. It is to some extent a reliable world, having density and duration. Its organisation can be surveyed and brought out again and again; gone over with closed eyes, and verified with open eyes. It is always there, next to your skin, if you look on it that way, cowering in your soul, if you prefer it so. It is your object, remains it as long as you wish, and remains a total stranger, within you and without. You perceive it, take it to yourself as the "truth," and it lets itself be taken; but it does not give itself to you. Only concerning it may you make yourself "understood" with others; it is ready, though attached to everyone in a different way, to be an object common to you all. But you cannot meet others in it. You cannot hold on to life without it, its reliability sustains you; but should you die in it, your grave would be in nothingness.

Or on the other hand, man meets what exists and becomes as what is over against him, always simply a *single* being and each thing simply as being. What exists is opened to him in happenings, and what happens affects him as what is. Nothing is present for him except this one being, but it implicates the whole world. Measure and comparison have disappeared; it lies with yourself how much of the immeasurable becomes reality for you. These meetings are not organised to make the world, but each is a sign of the world-order. They are not linked up with one another, but each assures you of your solidarity with the world. The world

which appears to you in this way is unreliable, for it takes on a
continually new appearance; you cannot hold it to its word. It has
no density, for everything in it penetrates everything else; no duration, for it comes even when it is not summoned, and vanishes
even when it is tightly held. It cannot be surveyed, and if you wish
to make it capable of survey you lose it. It comes, and comes to
bring *you* out; if it does not reach you, meet you, then it vanishes;
but it comes back in another form. It is not outside you, it stirs in
the depth of you; if you say "Soul of my soul" you have not said
too much. But guard against wishing to remove it into your soul—
for then you annihilate it. It is your present; only while you have it
do you have the present. You can make it into an object for yourself, to experience and to use; you must continually do this—and
as you do it you have no more present. Between you and it there is
mutual giving: you say *Thou* to it and give yourself to it, it says
Thou to you and gives itself to you. You cannot make yourself
understood with others concerning it, you are alone with it. But it
teaches you to meet others, and to hold your ground when you
meet them. Through the graciousness of its comings and the
solemn sadness of its goings it leads you away to the *Thou* in
which the parallel lines of relations meet. It does not help to sus-
tain you in life, it only helps you to glimpse eternity.

✦

The world of *It* is set in the context of space and time.

The world of *Thou* is not set in the context of either of these.

The particular *Thou*, after the relational event has run its
course, is *bound* to become an *It*.

The particular *It*, by entering the relational event, *may* become
a *Thou*.

These are the two basic privileges of the world of *It*. They
move man to look on the world of *It* as the world in which he has
to live, and in which it is comfortable to live, as the world, indeed,
which offers him all manner of incitements and excitements,

activity and knowledge. In this chronicle of solid benefits the moments of the *Thou* appear as strange lyric and dramatic episodes, seductive and magical, but tearing us away to dangerous extremes, loosening the well-tried context, leaving more questions than satisfaction behind them, shattering security—in short, uncanny moments we can well dispense with. For since we are bound to leave them and go back into the "world," why not remain in it? Why not call to order what is over against us, and send it packing into the realm of objects? Why, if we find ourselves on occasion with no choice but to say *Thou* to father, wife, or comrade, not say *Thou* and mean *It*? To utter the sound *Thou* with the vocal organs is by no means the same as saying the uncanny primary word; more, it is harmless to whisper with the soul an amorous *Thou,* so long as nothing else in a serious way is meant but *experience* and *make use of.*

It is not possible to live in the bare present. Life would be quite consumed if precautions were not taken to subdue the present speedily and thoroughly. But it is possible to live in the bare past, indeed only in it may a life be organised. We only need to fill each moment with experiencing and using, and it ceases to burn.

And in all the seriousness of truth, hear this: without *It* man cannot live. But he who lives with *It* alone is not a man.

Part Two

THE HISTORY OF THE INDIVIDUAL and that of the human race, in whatever they may continually part company, agree at least in this one respect, that they indicate a progressive augmentation of the world of *It*.

In respect of the history of the race that is called in question; it is pointed out that the successive realms of culture have their beginning in a primitive state, whose colour may differ, but whose structure is constant. In conformity with this primitiveness these cultural realms begin with a small world of objects. The life not of the race but of the particular culture would thus correspond to the individual life. But, apart from the apparently isolated realms, through the historical influence of other pre-existing cultures they take over, at a certain stage, the world of *It* belonging to these cultures. This stage is not reached early, but nevertheless precedes the generation of the heyday. It may take the form of direct acceptance of what is contemporary, as Greece accepted the Egyptian world; or it may take the form of indirect acceptance of what is past, as western Christianity accepted the Greek world. These cultures, then, enlarge their world of *It* not merely through their own experience, but also through the absorption of foreign experience. Only then does a culture, thus grown, fulfil itself in decisive, discovering expansion. (For the present let the paramount contribution made by the perception and acts of the world of *Thou* be left out of account.) Hence, in general, the world of objects in every culture is more extensive than that of its predecessor. Despite sundry stoppages and apparent retrogressions the progressive augmentation of the world of *It* is to be clearly discerned in history. It is beside the point of this conclusion whether the character of finitude or that of so-called infinity, more precisely non-finitude, belongs to the "world-view" of a culture; though certainly a "finite" world can well contain more parts, things, and processes than an "infinite." It is also to be observed that it is important to compare not merely the extent of natural knowledge, but also that of social differentiation and that of technical achievement. For through both of these the world of objects is enlarged.

The primary connexion of man with the world of *It* is comprised in *experiencing*, which continually reconstitutes the world, and *using*, which leads the world to its manifold aim, the sustaining, relieving, and equipping of human life. In proportion to the growing extent of the world of *It*, ability to experience and use it must also grow. The individual can, to be sure, more and more replace direct with indirect experience, he can "acquire items of knowledge," and he can more and more reduce his using of the world to specialised "utilisation"; nevertheless, a continual development of this ability, from generation to generation, cannot be avoided. This is the usual meaning of the talk about a progressive development of the spiritual life. By this talk, guilt of the real sin of speech against the spirit is undoubtedly incurred; for that "spiritual life" is for the most part the obstacle to a life lived in the spirit, and at best the material which, after being mastered and fashioned, is to go to make that life.

It is the obstacle; for the development of the ability to experience and use comes about mostly through the decrease of man's power to enter into relation—the power in virtue of which alone man can live the life of the spirit.

◆

SPIRIT IN ITS HUMAN MANIFESTATION is a response of man to his *Thou*. Man speaks with many tongues, tongues of language, of art, of action; but the spirit is one, the response to the *Thou* which appears and addresses him out of the mystery. Spirit is the word. And just as talk in a language may well first take the form of words in the brain of the man, and then sound in his throat, and yet both are merely refractions of the true event, for in actuality speech does not abide in man, but man takes his stand in speech and talks from there; so with every word and every spirit. Spirit is not in the *I*, but between *I* and *Thou*. It is not like the blood that circulates in you, but like the air in which you breathe. Man lives in the spirit, if he is able to respond to his *Thou*. He is able to, if he enters into relation with his whole being. Only in virtue of his power to enter into relation is he able to live in the spirit.

But the destiny of the relational event is here set forth in the most powerful way. The stronger the response the more strongly does it bind up the *Thou* and banish it to be an object. Only silence before the *Thou*—silence of *all* tongues, silent patience in the undivided word that precedes the formed and vocal response—leaves the *Thou* free, and permits man to take his stand with it in the reserve where the spirit is not manifest, but *is*. Every response binds up the *Thou* in the world of *It*. That is the melancholy of man, and his greatness. For that is how knowledge comes about, a work is achieved, and image and symbol made, in the midst of living beings.

But that which has been so changed into *It*, hardened into a thing among things, has had the nature and disposition put into it to change back again and again. This was the meaning in that hour of the spirit when spirit was joined to man and bred the response in him—again and again that which has the status of object must blaze up into presentness and enter the elemental state from which it came, to be looked on and lived in the present by men.

The fulfilment of this nature and disposition is thwarted by the man who has come to terms with the world of *It* that it is to be experienced and used. For now instead of freeing that which is bound up in that world he suppresses it, instead of looking at it he observes it, instead of accepting it as it is, he turns it to his own account.

Take knowledge: being is disclosed to the man who is engaged in knowing, as he looks at what is over against him. He will, indeed, have to grasp as an object that which he has seen with the force of presence, he will have to compare it with objects, establish it in its order among classes of objects, describe and analyse it objectively. Only as *It* can it enter the structure of knowledge. But when he saw it, it was no thing among things, no event among events, but exclusively present. Being did not share itself with him in terms of the law that was afterwards elicited from the appearance, but in terms of its very self. When a man thinks a general thought in this connexion he is merely unravelling the tangled incident; for it was seen in particular form, in what was over against him. Now the incident is included in the *It* of knowledge which is composed of ideas. He who frees it from that, and looks on it again in the present moment, fulfils the nature of the act of knowledge to be real and effective *between* men. But knowledge can also be managed in such a way that it is affirmed that "this, then, is how the matter stands, the thing is called this, made in this way, its place is over there"; that which has become *It* is left as *It*, experienced and used as *It*, appropriated for the undertaking to "find one's bearings" in the world, and then to "conquer" it.

So too in art: form is disclosed to the artist as he looks at what is over against him. He banishes it to be a "structure." This "structure" is not in a world of gods, but in this great world of men. It is certainly "there," even if no human eye seeks it out; but it is asleep. The Chinese poet tells how men did not wish to hear the tune he played on his jade flute; then he played it to the gods, and they inclined their ears; since then men also listened to the tune: thus he went from the gods to those whom the "structure" cannot dispense with. It longs as in a dream for the meeting with man, that for a timeless moment he may lift the ban and clasp the form. Then he comes on his way, and experiences what there is to be experienced: it is made in this way, or this is expressed in it, or its qualities are such and such, and further, it takes this place in the scheme of things.

It is not as though scientific and æsthetic understanding were not necessary; but they are necessary to man that he may do his work with precision and plunge it in the truth of relation, which is above the understanding and gathers it up in itself.

And, thirdly, there is pure effective action without arbitrary self-will. This is higher than the spirit of knowledge and the spirit of art, for here the mortal bodily man does not need to mix himself with the more lasting stuff, but himself outlasts it as structure; encircled by the sounding music of his living speech he reaches the starry heaven of the spirit. Here the *Thou* appeared to the man out of deeper mystery, addressed him even out of the darkness, and he responded with his life. Here the word has from time to time become life, and this life is *teaching*. This life may have fulfilled the law or broken it; both are continually necessary, that spirit may not die on earth. This life is presented, then, to those who come later, to teach them not what is and must be, but how life is lived in the spirit, face to face with the *Thou*. That is, it is itself ready on every occasion to become *Thou* for them, and open up the world of *Thou*—no; it is not ready: it continually approaches and touches them. But they, having become disinclined and unfitted for the living dealings that would open the world to them, are fully equipped with information. They have pinned the person down in history, and secured his words in the library. They have codified, in exactly the same way, the fulfilment or the breaking of the law. Nor are they niggards with admiration and even idolatry, amply mixed with psychology, as befits modern man. O lonely Face like a star in the night, o living Finger laid on an unheeding brow, o fainter echoing footstep!

◆

THE DEVELOPMENT of the function of experiencing and using comes about mostly through decrease of man's power to enter into relation.

How does this same man, who made spirit into a means of enjoyment for himself, behave towards the beings that live round about him?

Taking his stand in the shelter of the primary word of separation, which holds off the *I* and the *It* from one another, he has divided his life with his fellow-men into two tidily circled-off provinces, one of institutions and the other of feelings—the province of *It* and the province of *I*.

Institutions are "outside," where all sorts of aims are pursued, where a man works, negotiates, bears influence, undertakes, concurs, organises, conducts business, officiates, preaches. They are the tolerably well-ordered and to some extent harmonious structure, in which, with the manifold help of men's brains and hands, the process of affairs is fulfilled.

Feelings are "within," where life is lived and man recovers from institutions. Here the spectrum of the emotions dances before the interested glance. Here a man's liking and hate and pleasure are indulged, and his pain if it is not too severe. Here he is at home, and stretches himself out in his rocking-chair.

Institutions are a complicated market-place, feelings a boudoir rich in ever-changing interests.

The boundary line, to be sure, is constantly in danger since the wanton feelings break in at times on the most objective institutions; but with united goodwill it may be restored.

Most difficult of all is the reliable drawing of the boundary line in the realms of so-called personal life. In marriage, for instance, the line is occasionally not to be fully drawn in any simple way; but in the end it is possible. In the realms of so-called public life it can be perfectly drawn. Let it be considered, for instance, how faultlessly, in the year of the parties and the groups with their "movements" which aimed at being above parties, the heaven-storming sessions on the one hand, and on the other hand business, creeping along the ground (smoothly like a machine or slovenly and organically), are separated from one another.

But the separated *It* of institutions is an animated clod without soul, and the separated *I* of feelings an uneasily fluttering soul-bird. Neither of them knows man: institutions know only the specimen, feelings only the "object"; neither knows the person, or mutual life. Neither of them knows the present: even the most up-to-date institutions know only the lifeless past that is over and done with, and even the most lasting feelings know only the flitting moment that has not yet come properly into being. Neither of them has access to real life. Institutions yield no public life, and feelings no personal life.

That institutions yield no public life is realised by increasing numbers, realised with increasing distress: this is the starting-point of the seeking need of the age. That feelings yield no personal life is understood only by a few. For the most personal life of all seems to reside in feelings, and if, like the modern man, you have learned to concern yourself wholly with your own feelings, despair at their unreality will not easily instruct you in a better way—for despair is also an interesting feeling.

The men who suffer distress in the realisation that institutions yield no public life have hit upon an expedient: institutions must be loosened, or dissolved, or burst asunder, by the feelings themselves; they must be given new life from the feelings, by the introduction into them of the "freedom of feeling." If the mechanical State, say, links together citizens alien to one another in their very being, without establishing, or promoting, a being together, let the State, these men say, be replaced by the community of love; and this community will arise when people, out of free, abundant feeling, approach and wish to live with one another. But it is not so. The true community does not arise through peoples having feelings for one another (though indeed not without it), but through, first, their taking their stand in living mutual relation with a living Centre, and, second, their being in living mutual relation with one another. The second has its source in the first, but is not given when the first alone is given. Living mutual relation includes feelings, but does not originate with them. The community is built up out of living mutual relation, but the builder is the living effective Centre.

Further, institutions of the so-called personal life cannot be given new life by free feeling (though indeed not without it). Marriage, for instance, will never be given new life except by that out of which true marriage always arises, the revealing by two people of the *Thou* to one another. Out of this a marriage is built up by the *Thou* that is neither of the *I*'s. This is the metaphysical and metapsychical factor of love to which feelings of love are mere accompaniments. He who wishes to give new life to marriage from another source is not essentially different from him who wishes to abolish it. Both clearly show that they no longer know the vital factor. And indeed, if in all the much discussed erotic philosophy of the age we were to leave out of account everything that involves experience in relation to the *I*, that is, every situation in which the one is not present to the other, given present status by it, but merely enjoys itself in the other—what then would be left?

True public and true personal life are two forms of connexion. In that they come into being and endure, feelings (the changing content) and institutions (the constant form) are necessary; but put together they do not create human life: this is done by the third, the central presence of the *Thou*, or rather, more truly stated, by the central *Thou* that has been received in the present.

✦

THE PRIMARY WORD *I–It* is not of evil—as matter is not of evil. It is of evil—as matter is, which presumes to have the quality of present being. If a man lets it have the mastery, the continually growing world of *It* overruns him and robs him of the reality of his own *I*, till the incubus over him and the ghost within him whisper to one another the confession of their non-salvation.

◆

—BUT IS THE COMMUNAL LIFE OF MODERN MAN not then of necessity sunk in the world of *It*? Can the two compartments of this life,
economics and State, with their present extent and completeness
of structure, be conceived to rest on any other basis but that of a
deliberate renunciation of all "directness," and a resolute rejection
of every court of appeal which is "alien," that is, which does not
arise from this sphere itself? And if it is the experiencing and
using *I* that rules here, the *I* that makes use of assets and work
done in economics, and strivings and opinions in politics, must
we not thank this unlimited mastery for the extensive and solid
structure of the great "objective" products in these two circles? Is
not, indeed, the productive greatness of the leading statesman and
the leading economist bound up with the fact that he looks on the
men with whom he has to deal not as bearers of the *Thou* that cannot be experienced but as centres of work and effort, whose particular capabilities it is his concern to estimate and utilise? Would
his world not fall in on him if, instead of adding up *He* and *He* and
He to make an *It,* he tried to calculate the sum of *Thou* and *Thou*
and *Thou*—which never yields anything but *Thou* again? Would
that not be to exchange formative mastery for fastidious dilettan-
tism, and illuminating reason for cloudy fanaticism? And if we
look from the leaders to the led, has not the very development in
the nature of modern work and possession destroyed almost every
trace of living with what is over against them—of significant relation? It would be absurd to wish to return on this development—
and if the absurd did come about, the enormous and nicely
balanced apparatus of this civilisation, which alone makes life possible for the enormous numbers of men that have grown with it,
would simultaneously be destroyed.

—Speechmaker, you speak too late. Just a little time ago you
would have been able to believe in your speech, now you no
longer can. For, a moment ago, you saw as I did, that the State is

no longer led; the stokers still pile in the coal, but the leaders have now only the semblance of control over the madly racing machines. And in this moment, as you speak, you can hear as I do that the levers of economics are beginning to sound in an unusual way; the masters smile at you with superior assurance, but death is in their hearts. They tell you they suited the apparatus to the circumstances, but you notice that from now on they can only suit themselves to the apparatus—so long, that is to say, as it permits them. Their speakers teach you that economics is entering on the State's inheritance, but you know that there is nothing to inherit except the tyranny of the exuberantly growing *It*, under which the *I*, less and less able to master, dreams on that it is the ruler.

The communal life of man can no more than man himself dispense with the world of *It*, over which the presence of the *Thou* moves like the spirit upon the face of the waters. Man's will to profit and to be powerful have their natural and proper effect so long as they are linked with, and upheld by, his will to enter into relation. There is no evil impulse till the impulse has been separated from the being; the impulse which is bound up with, and defined by, the being is the living stuff of communal life, that which is detached is its disintegration. Economics, the abode of the will to profit, and State, the abode of the will to be powerful, share in life as long as they share in the spirit. If they abjure spirit they abjure life. Life, to be sure, gives itself time to bring its affairs to a real conclusion, and for a good while men imagine they see a structure moving where for a long time a machine has been whirling. The matter is indeed not to be helped by the introduction of a little directness. The loosening of the structure of economics or of the State cannot compensate for their being no longer under the dominance of the spirit that says *Thou:* no disturbance on the periphery can serve as substitute for the living relation with the Centre. Structures of man's communal life draw their living quality from the riches of the power to enter into relation, which penetrates their various parts, and obtain their bodily

form from the binding up of this power in the spirit. The statesman or the economist who obeys the spirit is no dilettante; he
knows well that he cannot, without undoing his work, simply
confront, as bearers of the *Thou,* the men with whom he has to
deal. Yet he risks doing it, not plainly and simply but as far as the
boundary set for him by the spirit. The spirit sets this for him,
and the risk that would have shattered a separated structure succeeds in the structure over which the presence of the *Thou*
broods. He is no fanatic; he serves the truth which, though
higher than reason, yet does not repudiate it, but holds it in its
lap. He does in communal life precisely what is done in personal
life by the man who knows himself incapable of realising the
Thou in its purity, yet daily confirms its truth in the *It,* in accordance with what is right and fitting for the day, drawing—disclos-
ing—the boundary line anew each day. So, too, only with spirit,
not themselves, as starting-point, are work and possession to be
released; only from the presence of spirit can meaning and joy
stream into all work, awe and sacrificial power into all possession—filling them not to the brim but sufficiently; only from its
presence can everything that is worked and possessed, while
remaining in adherence to the world of *It,* yet be transfigured into
what is over against man—into the representation of the *Thou.*
There is no going backwards, but in the very moment of deepest
need a hitherto undreamt-of movement forwards and outwards.

It does not matter if the State rules economics or is given its
authority by it, so long as both are unchanged. It does matter if
the organisation of the State becomes freer and that of economics
more equitable—but not for the question asked here about the
real life; they certainly cannot become free and equitable with
themselves as starting-point. It matters most of all if the spirit
which says *Thou,* which responds, remains by life and reality, if
that which is still interleaved by spirit in man's communal life is
subjected to the State and to economics or is independently
effective, and if that of spirit which still persists in man's personal

life is reassimilated into the communal life. If communal life were parcelled out into independent realms, one of which is "the spiritual life," this would certainly not be done; that would only mean to give up once and for all to tyranny the provinces that are sunk in the world of *It*, and to rob the spirit completely of reality. For the spirit is never independently effective in life in itself alone, but in relation to the world: possessing power that permeates the world of *It*, transforming it.

The spirit is truly "in its own realm" if it can confront the world that is unlocked to it, give itself to this world, and in its relation with it save both itself and the world. The distracted, weakened, degenerated, contradictory spirituality which to-day represents spirit would be able to do this only if it were to reach again the life of spirit which can utter the *Thou*.

◆

CAUSALITY HAS AN UNLIMITED REIGN in the world of *It*. Every "physical" event that can be perceived by the senses, but also every "psychical" event existing or discovered in self-experience is necessarily valid as being caused and as causing. Further, events to which a teleological character may be attributed are as parts of the unbroken world of *It* not excepted from this causality; the continuum to which they belong certainly tolerates a teleology, but only as the reverse side worked into a part of causality, and not impairing its continuity and completeness.

The unlimited reign of causality in the world of *It*, of fundamental importance for the scientific ordering of nature, does not weigh heavily on man, who is not limited to the world of *It*, but can continually leave it for the world of relation. Here *I* and *Thou* freely confront one another in mutual effect that is neither connected with nor coloured by any causality. Here man is assured of the freedom both of his being and of Being. Only he who knows relation and knows about the presence of the *Thou* is capable of decision. He who decides is free, for he has approached the Face.

The fiery stuff of all my ability to will seethes tremendously, all that I might do circles around me, still without actuality in the world, flung together and seemingly inseparable, alluring glimpses of powers flicker from all the uttermost bounds: the universe is my temptation, and I achieve being in an instant, with both hands plunged deep in the fire, where the single deed is hidden, the deed which aims at me—now is the moment! Already the menace of the abyss is removed, the centreless Many no longer plays in the iridescent sameness of its pretensions; but only two alternatives are set side by side—the other, the vain idea, and the one, the charge laid on me. But now realisation begins in me. For it is not decision to do the one and leave the other a lifeless mass, deposited layer upon layer as dross in my soul. But he alone who directs the whole strength of the alternative into the doing of the charge, who lets the abundant passion of what is rejected invade the growth to reality of what is chosen—he alone who "serves God with the evil impulse" makes decision, decides the event. If this is understood, it is also known that this which has been set up, towards which direction is set and decision made, is to be given the name of upright; and if there were a devil it would not be one who decided against God, but one who, in eternity, came to no decision.

Causality does not weigh on the man to whom freedom is assured. He knows that his mortal life swings by nature between *Thou* and *It*, and he is aware of the significance of this. It suffices him to be able to cross again and again the threshold of the holy place wherein he was not able to remain; the very fact that he must leave it again and again is inwardly bound up for him with the meaning and character of this life. There, on the threshold, the response, the spirit, is kindled ever new within him; here, in an unholy and needy country, this spark is to be proved. What is called necessity here cannot frighten him, for he has recognised there true necessity, namely, destiny.

Destiny and freedom are solemnly promised to one another. Only the man who makes freedom real to himself meets destiny. In my discovery of the deed that aims at me—in this movement of my freedom the mystery is revealed to me; but also in failure to fulfil the deed as I intended it to be—in this resistance, too, the mystery is revealed to me. He who forgets all that is caused and makes decision out of the depths, who rids himself of property and raiment and naked approaches the Face, is a free man, and destiny confronts him as the counterpart of his freedom. It is not his boundary, but his fulfilment; freedom and destiny are linked together in meaning. And in this meaning destiny, with eyes a moment ago so severe now filled with light, looks out like grace itself.

No; causal necessity does not weigh heavily on the man who returns to the world of *It* bearing this spark. And in times of healthy life trust streams from men of the spirit to all people. To all men indeed, even to the dullest, meeting—the present—has come somehow, naturally, impulsively, dimly: all men have somewhere been aware of the *Thou;* now the spirit gives them full assurance.

But in times of sickness it comes about that the world of *It,* no longer penetrated and fructified by the inflowing world of *Thou* as by living streams but separated and stagnant, a gigantic ghost of the fens, overpowers man. In coming to terms with a world of objects that no longer assume present being for him he succumbs to this world. Then smooth causality rises up till it is an oppressive, stifling fate.

Every great culture that comprehends nations rests on an original relational incident, on a response to the *Thou* made at its source, on an act of the being made by the spirit. This act, strengthened by the similarly directed power of succeeding generations, creates in the spirit a special conception of the cosmos; only through this act is cosmos, an apprehended world, a world that is homely and houselike, man's dwelling in the world, made possible again and again. Only now can man, confident in his soul, build again and again, in a special conception of space, dwellings for God and dwellings for men, and fill swaying time with new hymns and songs, and shape the very community of men. But he is free and consequently creative only so long as he possesses, in action and suffering in his own life, that act of the being—so long as he himself enters into relation. If a culture ceases to be centred in the living and continually renewed relational event, then it hardens into the world of *It*, which the glowing deeds of solitary spirits only spasmodically break through. Thenceforth smooth causality, which before had no power to disturb the spiritual conception of the cosmos, rises up till it is an oppressive, stifling fate. Wise and masterful destiny, that reigned, in harmony with the wealth of meaning in the cosmos, over all causality, has been changed into a demonic spirit adverse to meaning, and has fallen into the power of causality. The very *karma* that appeared to the forefathers as a charitable dispensation—for what we do in this life raises us up for a future life in higher spheres—is now recognised as tyranny: for the *karma* of an earlier life of which we are unconscious has shut us in a prison we cannot break in this life. Where hitherto a heaven was established in a law, manifest to the senses, raising its light arch from which the spindle of necessity hangs, the wandering stars now rule in senseless and oppressive might. It was necessary only to give oneself to Dike, the heavenly "way," which means also our way, in order to dwell with free heart in the universal bounds of fate. But now, whatever we do, we are laden with the whole burden of the dead weight of the world, with fate that does not know spirit. The storming desire for salvation is unsatisfied after manifold attempts, till it is stilled by one who learns to escape the cycle of births, or by one who saves the souls, that have fallen to alien powers, into the freedom of the children of God. Such an achievement arises out of a new event of meeting, which is in the course of assuming substantial being—out of a new response, determining destiny, of a man to his *Thou*. In the working out of this central act of the being, one culture can be relieved by another that is given up to the influence of this act, but it can also be given new life in itself alone.

The sickness of our age is like that of no other age, and it belongs together with them all. The history of cultures is not a course of æons in which one runner after another has to traverse gaily and unsuspectingly the same death-track. A nameless way runs through their rise and fall: not a way of progress and development, but a spiral descent through the spiritual underworld, which can also be called an ascent to the innermost, finest, most complicated whirlpool, where there is no advance and no retreat, but only utterly new reversal—the break through. Shall we have to go this way to the end, to trial of the final darkness? Where there is danger, the rescuing force grows too.

The quasi-biological and quasi-historical thought of to-day, however different the aims of each, have worked together to establish a more tenacious and oppressive belief in fate than has ever before existed. The might of *karma* or of the stars no longer controls inevitably the lot of man; many powers claim the mastery, but rightly considered most of our contemporaries believe in a mixture of them, just as the late Romans believed in a mixture of gods. This is made easier by the nature of the claim. Whether it is the "law of life" of a universal struggle in which all must take part or renounce life, or the "law of the soul" which completely builds up the psychical person from innate habitual instincts, or the "social law" of an irresistible social process to which will and consciousness may only be accompaniments, or the "cultural law" of an unchangeably uniform coming and going of historical structures— whatever form it takes, it always means that man is set in the frame of an inescapable happening that he cannot, or can only in his frenzy, resist. Consecration in the mysteries brought freedom from the compulsion of the stars, and brahman-sacrifice with its accompanying knowledge brought freedom from the compulsion of *karma:* in both redemption was represented. But the composite god tolerates no belief in release. It is considered folly to imagine any freedom; there is only one choice, between resolute, and hopeless rebellious, slavery. And no matter how much is said, in all these laws, of teleological development and organic growth, at the basis of them all lies possession by process, that is by unlimited causality. The dogma of gradual process is the abdication of man before the exuberant world of *It*. He misuses the name of destiny: destiny is not a dome pressed tightly down on the world of men; no one meets it but he who went out from freedom. But the dogma of process leaves no room for freedom, none for its most real revelation of all, whose calm strength changes the face of the earth: turning. This dogma does not know the man who through reversal surmounts the universal struggle, tears to pieces the web of habitual instincts, raises the class ban, and stirs, rejuvenates, and transforms the stable structures of history. This dogma allows you in its game only the choice to observe the rules or to retire: but he who is turning overthrows the pieces. The dogma is always willing to allow you to fulfil its limitation with your life and "to remain free" in your soul; but he who is turning looks on this freedom as the most ignominious bondage.

The only thing that can become fate for a man is belief in fate; for this suppresses the movement of turning.

Belief in fate is mistaken from the beginning. All consideration in terms of process is merely an ordering of pure "having become," of the separated world-event, of objectivity as though it were history; the presence of the *Thou*, the becoming out of solid connexion, is inaccessible to it. It does not know the reality of spirit; its scheme is not valid for spirit. Prediction from objectivity is valid only for the man who does not know presentness. He who is overcome by the world of *It* is bound to see, in the dogma of immutable process, a truth that clears a way through the exuberant growth; in very truth this dogma enslaves him only the more deeply to the world of *It*. But the world of *Thou* is not closed. He who goes out to it with concentrated being and risen power to enter into relation becomes aware of freedom. And to be freed from belief that there is no freedom is indeed to be free.

◆

AS POWER OVER THE INCUBUS is obtained by addressing it with its real name, so the world of *It*, which a moment ago was stretched in its uncanniness before the puny strength of men, is bound to yield to the man who knows it for what it really is—severance and alienation of that out of whose abundance, when it streams close at hand, every earthly *Thou* is met, and of that which, though seeming at times great and fearful like the mother-god, yet always had a motherly air.

—But how can the man in whose being lurks a ghost, the *I* emptied of reality, muster the strength to address the incubus by name? How can the ruined power in a being to enter into relation be raised again, when an active ghost tramples continually on the ruins? How does a being gather itself together, that is madly and unceasingly hunted in an empty circle by the separated *I*? How may a man who lives in arbitrary self-will become aware of freedom?

—As freedom and destiny, so arbitrary self-will and fate belong together. But freedom and destiny are solemnly promised to one another and linked together in meaning; while arbitrary self-will and fate, soul's spectre and world's nightmare, endure one another, living side by side and avoiding one another, without connexion or conflict, in meaninglessness—till in an instant there is confused shock of glance on glance, and confession of their non-redemption breaks from them. How much eloquent and ingenious spirituality is expended to-day in the effort to avert, or at least to veil, this event!

The free man is he who wills without arbitrary self-will. He believes in reality, that is, he believes in the real solidarity of the real twofold entity *I* and *Thou*. He believes in destiny, and believes that it stands in need of him. It does not keep him in leading-strings, it awaits him, he must go to it, yet does not know where it is to be found. But he knows that he must go out with his whole being. The matter will not turn out according to his decision; but what is to come will come only when he decides on what he is able to will. He must sacrifice his puny, unfree will, that is controlled by things and instincts, to his grand will, which quits defined for destined being. Then he intervenes no more, but at the same time he does not let things merely happen. He listens to what is emerging from himself, to the course of being in the world; not in order to be supported by it, but in order to bring it to reality as it desires, in its need of him, to be brought—with human spirit and deed, human life and death. I said *he believes,* but that really means *he meets.*

The self-willed man does not believe and does not meet. He does not know solidarity of connexion, but only the feverish world outside and his feverish desire to use it. Use needs only to be given an ancient name, and it companies with the gods. When this man says *Thou,* he means "O my ability to use," and what he terms his destiny is only the equipping and sanctioning of his ability to use. He has in truth no destiny, but only a being that is defined by things and instincts, which he fulfils with the feeling of sovereignty—that is, in the arbitrariness of self-will. He has no grand will, only self-will, which he passes off as real will. He is wholly incapable of sacrifice, even though he may have the word on his lips; you know him by the fact that the word never becomes concrete. He intervenes continually, and that for the purpose of "letting things happen." Why should destiny, he says to you, not be given a helping hand? Why should the attainable means required by such a purpose not be utilised? He sees the free man, too, in this way; he can see him in no other. But the free man has no purpose here and means there, which he fetches for his purpose: he has only the one thing, his repeated decision to approach his destiny. He has made this decision, and from time to time, at every parting of ways, he will renew it. But he could sooner believe he was not alive than that the decision of his grand will was inadequate and needed to be supported by a means. He believes; he meets. But the unbelieving core in the self-willed man can perceive nothing but unbelief and self-will, establishing of a purpose and devising of a means. Without sacrifice and without grace, without meeting and without presentness, he has as his world a mediated world cluttered with purposes. His world cannot be anything else, and its name is fate. Thus with all his sovereignty he is wholly and inextricably entangled in the unreal. He knows this whenever he turns his thoughts to himself; that is why he directs the best part of his spirituality to averting or at least to veiling his thoughts.

But these thoughts about apostasy, about the *I* emptied of reality and the real *I,* thoughts of letting oneself sink and take root in the soil called despair by men, soil out of which arise self-destruction and re-birth, would be the beginning of turning.

◆

ONCE UPON A TIME, tells the Brahmana of the hundred paths, gods and demons were at strife. The demons said: "To whom can we bring our offerings?" They set them all in their own mouths. But the gods set the gifts in one another's mouths. Then Prajapati, the primal spirit, gave himself to the gods.

◆

—IT IS UNDERSTANDABLE that the word of *It,* given over to itself, that is, not brought into contact with and melted down by the *Thou* as it comes into being, takes on the alien form of an incubus. But how is it that (as you say) the *I* of man is emptied of reality? Surely, whether living in or out of relation, the *I* is assured of itself through its self-consciousness, that strong golden thread on which the many-coloured circumstances are strung. If now *I* say, "I see you," or, "I see the tree," perhaps the seeing is not real in the same way in both, but the *I* in both is real in the same way.

—Let us make trial if this is so. The form of the words proves nothing. If many a spoken *Thou* indicates fundamentally an *It,* addressed as *Thou* only from habit and obtuseness, and many a spoken *It* fundamentally a *Thou,* its presentness remembered as it were remotely with the whole being, so are countless *I*'s only indispensable pronouns, necessary abbreviations for "This man here who is speaking." You speak of self-consciousness? If in the one sentence the *Thou* of relation is truly meant and in the other the *It* of an experience, that is, if the *I* in both is truly meant, is it the same *I* out of whose self-consciousness both are spoken?

The *I* of the primary word *I–Thou* is a different *I* from that of the primary word *I–It*.

The *I* of the primary word *I–It* makes its appearance as individuality and becomes conscious of itself as subject (of experiencing and using).

The *I* of the primary word *I–Thou* makes its appearance as person and becomes conscious of itself as subjectivity (without a dependent genitive).

Individuality makes its appearance by being differentiated from other individualities.

A person makes his appearance by entering into relation with other persons.

The one is the spiritual form of natural detachment, the other the spiritual form of natural solidarity of connexion.

The aim of self-differentiation is to experience and to use, and the aim of these is "life," that is, dying that lasts the span of a man's life.

The aim of relation is relation's own being, that is, contact with the *Thou*. For through contact with every *Thou* we are stirred with a breath of the *Thou*, that is, of eternal life.

He who takes his stand in relation shares in a reality, that is, in a being that neither merely belongs to him nor merely lies outside him. All reality is an activity in which I share without being able to appropriate for myself. Where there is no sharing there is no reality. Where there is self-appropriation there is no reality. The more direct the contact with the *Thou*, the fuller is the sharing.

The *I* is real in virtue of its sharing in reality. The fuller its sharing the more real it becomes.

But the *I* that steps out of the relational event into separation and consciousness of separation, does not lose its reality. Its sharing is preserved in it in a living way. In other words, as is said of the supreme relation and may be used of all, "the seed remains in it." This is the province of subjectivity in which the *I* is aware with a single awareness of its solidarity of connexion and of its separation. Genuine subjectivity can only be dynamically understood, as the swinging of the *I* in its lonely truth. Here, too, is the place where the desire is formed and heightened for ever higher, more unconditioned relation, for the full sharing in being. In subjectivity the spiritual substance of the person matures.

The person becomes conscious of himself as sharing in being, as co-existing, and thus as being. Individuality becomes conscious of itself as being such-and-such and nothing else. The person says, "I am," the individual says, "I am such-and-such." "Know thyself," means for the person "know thyself to have being," for the individual it means "know thy particular kind of being." Individuality in differentiating itself from others is rendered remote from true being.

We do not mean by this that the person in any way "gives up" his special being, his being different—only that this being is not his observation-point, but simply there, the necessary and significant conception of being. Individuality, on the other hand, revels in its special being or, rather, mostly in the fiction of its special being which it has made up for itself. For to know itself means basically for it (for the most part) to establish an authoritative apparent self, capable of deceiving it ever more and more fundamentally, and to procure for itself, in looking to and honouring this apparent self, the semblance of knowledge of its own being as it really is. Real knowledge of its being would lead it to self-destruction—or to rebirth.

The person looks on his Self, individuality is concerned with its My—my kind, my race, my creation, my genius.

Individuality neither shares in nor obtains any reality. It differentiates itself from the other, and seeks through experiencing and using to appropriate as much of it as it can. This is *its* dynamic, self-differentiation and appropriation, each exercised on the *It* within the unreal. The subject, as it thinks itself to be, may make as much as it likes into its own; in virtue of this it acquires no substance, but remains a functional point, experiencing and using, no more. None of its extensive and manifold defined being and none of its zealous "individuality" can help it to win substance.

There are not two kinds of man, but two poles of humanity.

No man is pure person and no man pure individuality. None is wholly real, and none wholly unreal. Every man lives in the twofold *I*. But there are men so defined by person that they may be called persons, and men so defined by individuality that they may be called individuals. True history is decided in the field between these two poles.

The more a man, humanity, is mastered by individuality, the deeper does the *I* sink into unreality. In such times the person in man and in humanity leads a hidden subterranean and as it were cancelled existence—till it is recalled.

◆

THE STRONGER THE *I* of the primary word *I–Thou* is in the twofold *I,* the more personal is the man.

According to his saying of *I*—according to what he means, when he says *I*—it can be decided where a man belongs and where his way leads. The word *I* is the true shibboleth of mankind.

So listen to this word!

How discordant the *I* of the individual! It may stir great compassion if it comes from lips compressed in the tragedy of concealed self-contradiction. It may rouse horror if it comes chaotically from lips that wildly, heedlessly, unsuspectingly, show forth the contradiction. If it comes idly and glibly it is painful or disagreeable.

He who speaks the separated *I,* with emphasis on the capital, lays here the shame of the world-spirit which has been degraded to spirituality.

But how lovely and how fitting the sound of the lively and impressive *I* of Socrates! It is the *I* of endless dialogue, and the air of dialogue is wafted around it in all its journeys, before the judges and in the last hour in prison. This *I* lived continually in the relation with man which is bodied forth in dialogue. It never ceased to believe in the reality of men, and went out to meet them. So it took its stand with them in reality, and reality forsakes it no more. Its very loneliness can never be forsakenness, and if the world of man is silent it hears the voice of the daimonion say *Thou.*

How lovely and how legitimate the sound of the full *I* of Goethe! It is the *I* of pure intercourse with nature; nature gives herself to it and speaks unceasingly with it, revealing her mysteries to it but not betraying her mystery. It believes in her, and says to the rose, "Then thou art it"—then it takes its stand with it in a single reality. So the spirit of the real remains with it when it turns back to itself, the gaze of the sun abides with the blessed eye that considers its own radiance, and the friendship of the elements accompanies the man into the stillness of dying and becoming.

This is the sound through the ages of the "sufficient, true, and pure" saying of the *I* by those persons who, like Socrates and Goethe, are, bound up in relation.

And to anticipate by taking an illustration from the realm of unconditional relation: how powerful, even to being overpowering, and how legitimate, even to being self-evident, is the saying of *I* by Jesus! For it is the *I* of unconditional relation in which the man calls his *Thou* Father in such a way that he himself is simply Son, and nothing else but Son. Whenever he says *I* he can only mean the *I* of the holy primary word that has been raised for him into unconditional being. If separation ever touches him, his solidarity of relation is the greater; he speaks to others only out of this solidarity. It is useless to seek to limit this *I* to a power in itself or this *Thou* to something dwelling in ourselves, and once again to empty the real, the present relation, of reality. *I* and *Thou* abide;

every man can say *Thou* and is then *I*, every man can say Father and is then Son: reality abides.

◆

—But how if a man's mission require him to know nothing but connexion with his particular Cause, that is, no longer to know any real relation with or present realisation of a *Thou*—to have everything about him become an *It*, serving his particular Cause? What of Napoleon's saying of the *I*? Is it not legitimate? Is this phenomenon of experiencing and using not a person?

—Indeed the lord of the age manifestly did not know the dimension of the *Thou*. It has been justly expressed in the words that all being was for him *valore*. He who indulgently compared with Peter the followers who denied him after his fall had no one whom he himself could have denied; for he had no one whom he recognised as a being. He was for millions the demonic *Thou*, the *Thou* that does not respond, that responds to *Thou* with *It*, that does not respond genuinely in the personal sphere but responds only in his own sphere, his particular Cause, with his own deeds. This demonic *Thou*, to which no one can become *Thou*, is the elementary barrier of history, where the basic word of connexion loses its reality, its character of mutual action. In addition to (not between) person and individual, free and self-willed man, there is this third, towering in times of destiny, fraught with destiny. Towards him everything flames, but his fire is cold. To him a thousand several relations lead, but from him none. He shares in no reality, but in him immeasurable share is taken as though in a reality.

He sees the beings around him, indeed, as machines, capable of various achievements, which must be taken into account and utilised for the Cause. In this way, too, he sees himself—except that he must continually ascertain anew by experiment his power of achievement (whose limits he does not experience): he treats himself, too, as an *It*.

Thus, then, his saying of *I* is not a lively impressive, not a full one; but it is all the less a saying (like that of the modern individual) that deceives about these things. He does not speak of himself, but only "with himself as starting-point." The *I* that he utters and writes is the necessary subject for the sentences of his determinations and arrangements—no more and no less. It has no subjectivity, but it has also no self-consciousness concerned with its defined being, and thus all the more no illusion of the apparent self. "I am the clock, which exists, and does not know itself"—so he himself expressed his destined being, the reality of this phenomenon and the unreality of this *I,* at the time when he was hurled from his Cause, and for the first time had, and dared, to speak and think of himself, and to take thought for his *I*—which now appeared for the first time. The *I* that appears is not a mere subject, but neither does it move towards subjectivity; freed from its enchantment, but not saved, it expresses itself in the fearful word that is as legitimate as it is illegitimate: "The universe beholds us!" In the end it sinks back in mystery.

Who would dare to assert, after such a course and such a fall, that this man understood his tremendous, prodigious mission— or that he misunderstood it? It is certain that the age, for which the demoniacal, without present, has become master and model, misunderstands him. It does not know that what rule here are not lust for power and enjoyment of power, but destiny and consummation. It grows enthusiastic over this despotic brow, and has no suspicion of what signs are written across it, like the figures on the face of the clock. It industriously imitates this way of looking on living beings, without understanding its need and its necessity, and exchanges the rigorous attention of this *I* to the particular business for excited self-consciousness. The word "I" remains the shibboleth of mankind. Napoleon spoke it without power to enter into relation, but he spoke it as the *I* of a consummation. He who strives to say it as he said it only betrays the desperateness of his own self-contradiction.

✦

—WHAT IS SELF-CONTRADICTION:

—If a man does not represent the *a priori* of relation in his living with the world, if he does not work out and realise the inborn *Thou* on what meets it, then it strikes inwards. It develops on the unnatural, impossible object of the *I,* that is, it develops where there is no place at all for it to develop. Thus confrontation of what is over against him takes place within himself, and this cannot be relation, or presence, or streaming interaction, but only self-contradiction. The man may seek to explain it as a relation, perhaps as a religious relation, in order to wrench himself from the horror of the inner double-ganger; but he is bound to discover again and again the deception in the explanation. Here is the verge of life, flight of an unfulfilled life to the senseless semblance of fulfilment, and its groping in a maze and losing itself ever more profoundly.

✦

AT TIMES THE MAN, shuddering at the alienation between the *I* and the world, comes to reflect that something is to be done. As when in the grave night-hour you lie, racked by waking dream—bulwarks have fallen away and the abyss is screaming—and note amid your torment: there is still life, if only I got through to it—but how, how?; so is this man in the hours of reflection, shuddering, and aimlessly considering this and that. And perhaps, away in the unloved knowledge of the depths within him, he really knows the direction of turning, leading through sacrifice. But he spurns this knowledge; "mysticism" cannot resist the sun of electric light. He calls thought, in which he rightly has great confidence, to his aid; it shall make good everything for him again. It is, in truth, the high art of thought to paint a reliable picture of the world that is even worthy of belief. So this man says to his thought, "You see this thing stretched out here with the cruel eyes—was it not my playfellow once? You know how it laughed at me then with these very eyes, and they had good in them then? And you see my wretched *I*—I will confess to you, it is empty, and whatever I do in myself, as a result of experiencing and using, does not fathom its emptiness. Will you make it up between me and it, so that it leaves off and I recover?" And thought, ready with its service and its art, paints with its well-known speed one— no, two rows of pictures, on the right wall and on the left. On the one there is (or rather, there takes place, for the world-pictures of thought are reliable cinematography) the universe. The tiny earth plunges from the whirling stars, tiny man from the teeming earth, and now history bears him further through the ages, to rebuild persistently the ant-hill of the cultures which history crushes underfoot. Beneath the row of pictures is written: "One and all." On the other wall there takes place the soul. A spinner is spinning the orbits of all stars and the life of all creation and the history of the universe; everything is woven on one thread, and is no longer called stars and creation and universe, but sensations and imaginings, or even experiences, and conditions of the soul. And beneath the row of pictures is written: "One and all."

Thenceforth, if ever the man shudders at the alienation, and the world strikes terror in his heart, he looks up (to right or left, just as it may chance) and sees a picture. There he sees that the *I* is embedded in the world and that there is really no *I* at all—so the world can do nothing to the *I*, and he is put at ease; or he sees that the world is embedded in the *I*, and that there is really no world at all—so the world can do nothing to the *I*, and he is put at ease. Another time, if the man shudders at the alienation, and the *I* strikes terror in his heart, he looks up and sees a picture; which picture he sees does not matter, the empty *I* is stuffed full with the world or the stream of the world flows over it, and he is put at ease.

But a moment comes, and it is near, when the shuddering man looks up and sees both pictures in a flash together. And a deeper shudder seizes him.

Part Three

———◆———

THE EXTENDED LINES OF RELATIONS meet in the eternal *Thou*.

Every particular *Thou* is a glimpse through to the eternal *Thou;* by means of every particular *Thou* the primary word addresses the eternal *Thou*. Through this mediation of the *Thou* of all beings fulfilment, and non-fulfilment, of relations comes to them: the inborn *Thou* is realised in each relation and consummated in none. It is consummated only in the direct relation with the *Thou* that by its nature cannot become *It*.

◆

MEN HAVE ADDRESSED THEIR ETERNAL *Thou* with many names. In singing of Him who was thus named they always had the *Thou* in mind: the first myths were hymns of praise. Then the names took refuge in the language of *It;* men were more and more strongly moved to think of and to address their eternal *Thou* as an *It*. But all God's names are hallowed, for in them He is not merely spoken about, but also spoken to.

Many men wish to reject the word God as a legitimate usage, because it is so misused. It is indeed the most heavily laden of all the words used by men. For that very reason it is the most imperishable and most indispensable. What does all mistaken talk about God's being and works (though there has been, and can be, no other talk about these) matter in comparison with the one truth that all men who have addressed God had God Himself in mind? For he who speaks the word God and really has *Thou* in mind (whatever the illusion by which he is held), addresses the true *Thou* of his life, which cannot be limited by another *Thou,* and to which he stands in a relation that gathers up and includes all others.

But when he, too, who abhors the name, and believes himself to be godless, gives his whole being to addressing the *Thou* of his life, as a *Thou* that cannot be limited by another, he addresses God.

◆

IF WE GO ON OUR WAY and meet a man who has advanced towards us and has also gone on *his* way, we know only our part of the way, not his—his we experience only in the meeting.

Of the complete relational event we know, with the knowledge of life lived, our going out to the relation, our part of the way. The other part only comes upon us, we do not know it; it comes upon us in the meeting. But we strain ourselves on it if we speak of it as though it were some thing beyond the meeting.

We have to be concerned, to be troubled, not about the other side but about our own side, not about grace but about will. Grace concerns us in so far as we go out to it and persist in its presence; but it is not our object.

The *Thou* confronts me. But I step into direct relation with it. Hence the relation means being chosen and choosing, suffering and action in one; just as any action of the whole being which means the suspension of all partial actions, and consequently of all sensations of actions grounded only in their particular limitation, is bound to resemble suffering.

This is the activity of the man who has become a whole being, an activity that has been termed doing nothing: nothing separate or partial stirs in the man any more, thus he makes no intervention in the world; it is the whole man, enclosed and at rest in his wholeness, that is effective—he has become an effective whole. To have won stability in this state is to be able to go out to the supreme meeting.

To this end the world of sense does not need to be laid aside as though it were illusory. There is no illusory world, there is only the world—which appears to us as twofold in accordance with our twofold attitude. Only the barrier of separation has to be destroyed. Further, no "going beyond sense-experience" is necessary; for every experience, even the most spiritual, could yield us only an *It*. Nor is any recourse necessary to a world of ideas and values; for they cannot become presentness for us. None of these things is necessary. Can it be said what really is necessary?—Not in the sense of a precept. For everything that has ever been devised and contrived in the time of the human spirit as precept, alleged preparation, practice, or meditation, has nothing to do with the primal, simple fact of the meeting. Whatever the advantages in knowledge or the wielding of power for which we have to thank this or that practice, none of this affects the meeting of which we are speaking; it all has its place in the world of *It* and does not lead one step, does not take *the* step, out of it. Going out to the relation cannot be taught in the sense of precepts being given. It can only be indicated by the drawing of a circle which excludes everything that is not this going out. Then the one thing that matters is visible, full acceptance of the present.

To be sure, this acceptance presupposes that the further a man has wandered in separated being the more difficult is the venture and the more elemental the turning. This does not mean a giving up of, say, the *I*, as mystical writings usually suppose: the *I* is as indispensable to this, the supreme, as to every relation, since relation is only possible between *I* and *Thou*. It is not the *I*, then, that is given up, but that false self-asserting instinct that makes a man flee to the possessing of things before the unreliable, perilous world of relation which has neither density nor duration and cannot be surveyed.

◆

EVERY REAL RELATION with a being or life in the world is exclusive. Its *Thou* is freed, steps forth, is single, and confronts you. It fills the heavens. This does not mean that nothing else exists; but all else lives in *its* light. As long as the presence of the relation continues, this its cosmic range is inviolable. But as soon as a *Thou* becomes *It,* the cosmic range of the relation appears as an offence to the world, its exclusiveness as an exclusion of the universe.

In the relation with God unconditional exclusiveness and unconditional inclusiveness are one. He who enters on the absolute relation is concerned with nothing isolated any more, neither things nor beings, neither earth nor heaven; but everything is gathered up in the relation. For to step into pure relation is not to disregard everything but to see everything in the *Thou,* not to renounce the world but to establish it on its true basis. To look away from the world, or to stare at it, does not help a man to reach God; but he who sees the world in Him stands in His presence. "Here world, there God" is the language of *It;* "God in the world" is another language of *It;* but to eliminate or leave behind nothing at all, to include the whole world in the *Thou,* to give the world its due and its truth, to include nothing beside God but everything in him—this is full and complete relation.

Men do not find God if they stay in the world. They do not find Him if they leave the world. He who goes out with his whole being to meet his *Thou* and carries to it all being that is in the world, finds Him who cannot be sought.

Of course God is the "wholly Other"; but He is also the wholly Same, the wholly Present. Of course He is the *Mysterium Tremendum* that appears and overthrows; but He is also the mystery of the self-evident, nearer to me than my *I.*

If you explore the life of things and of conditioned being you come to the unfathomable, if you deny the life of things and of conditioned being you stand before nothingness, if you hallow this life you meet the living God.

✦

MAN'S SENSE OF *Thou*, which experiences in the relations with every particular *Thou* the disappointment of the change to *It*, strives out but not away from them all to its eternal *Thou;* but not as something is sought: actually there is no such thing as seeking God, for there is nothing in which He could not be found. How foolish and hopeless would be the man who turned aside from the course of his life in order to seek God; even though he won all the wisdom of solitude and all the power of concentrated being he would miss God. Rather is it as when a man goes his way and simply wishes that it might be the way: in the strength of his wish his striving is expressed. Every relational event is a stage that affords him a glimpse into the consummating event. So in each event he does not partake, but also (for he is waiting) does partake, of the one event. Waiting, not seeking, he goes his way; hence he is composed before all things, and makes contact with them which helps them. But when he has *found*, his heart is not turned from them, though everything now meets him in the one event. He blesses every cell that sheltered him, and every cell into which he will yet turn. For this finding is not the end, but only the eternal middle, of the way.

It is a finding without seeking, a discovering of the primal, of origin. His sense of *Thou*, which cannot be satiated till he finds the endless *Thou*, had the *Thou* present to it from the beginning; the presence had only to become wholly real to him in the reality of the hallowed life of the world.

God cannot be inferred in anything—in nature, say, as its author, or in history as its master, or in the subject as the self that is thought in it. Something else is not "given" and God then elicited from it; but God is the Being that is directly, most nearly, and lastingly, over against us, that may properly only be addressed, not expressed.

◆

MEN WISH TO REGARD A FEELING (called feeling of dependence, and recently, more precisely, creaturely feeling) as the real element in the relation with God. In proportion as the isolation and definition of this element is accurate, its unbalanced emphasis only makes the character of complete relation the more misunderstood.

What has already been said of love is even more unshakably valid here. Feelings are a mere accompaniment to the metaphysical and metapsychical fact of the relation, which is fulfilled not in the soul but between *I* and *Thou*. A feeling may be considered ever so essential, it remains nevertheless subject to the dynamic of the soul, where one feeling is outstripped, outdone, and abolished by another. In distinction from relation a feeling has its place in a scale. But above all, every feeling has its place within a polar tension, obtaining its colour and significance not from itself alone, but also from the opposite pole: every feeling is conditioned by its opposite. Thus the absolute relation (which gathers up into reality all those that are relative, and is no more a part, as these are, but is the whole that completes and unifies them all), in being reduced to the status of an isolated and limited feeling, is made into a relative psychological matter.

If the soul is the starting-point of our consideration, complete relation can be understood only in a bipolar way, only as the *coincidentia oppositorum*, as the coincidence of oppositions of feeling. Of course, the one pole—suppressed by the person's basic religious attitude—often disappears from the reflective consciousness, and can only be recalled in the purest and most ingenuous consideration of the depths of the being.

Yes; in pure relation you have felt yourself to be simply dependent, as you are able to feel in no other relation—and simply free, too, as in no other time or place: you have felt yourself to be both creaturely and creative. You had the one feeling then no longer limited by the other, but you had both of them limitlessly and together.

You know always in your heart that you need God more than everything; but do you not know too that God needs you—in the fulness of His eternity needs you? How would man be, how would you be, if God did not need him, did not need you? You need God, in order to be—and God needs you, for the very meaning of your life. In instruction and in poems men are at pains to say more, and they say too much—what turgid and presumptuous talk that is about the "God who becomes"; but we know unshakably in our hearts that there is a becoming of the God that is. The world is not divine sport, it is divine destiny. There is divine meaning in the life of the world, of man, of human persons, of you and of me.

Creation happens to us, burns itself into us, recasts us in burning—we tremble and are faint, we submit. We take part in creation, meet the Creator, reach out to Him, helpers and companions.

Two great servants pace through the ages, prayer and sacrifice. The man who prays pours himself out in unrestrained dependence, and knows that he has—in an incomprehensible way—an effect upon God, even though he obtains nothing from God; for when he no longer desires anything for himself he sees the flame of his effect burning at its highest.—And the man who makes sacrifice?—I cannot despise him, this upright servant of former times, who believed that God yearned for the scent of his burnt-offering. In a foolish but powerful way he knew that we can and ought to give to God. This is known by him, too, who offers up his little will to God and meets Him in the grand will. "Thy will be done," he says, and says no more; but truth adds for him, "through me whom *Thou* needest."

What distinguishes sacrifice and prayer from all magic?—Magic desires to obtain its effects without entering into relation, and practises its tricks in the void. But sacrifice and prayer are set "before the Face," in the consummation of the holy primary word that means mutual action: they speak the *Thou,* and then they hear.

To wish to understand pure relation as dependence is to wish to empty one of the bearers of the relation, and hence the relation itself, of reality.

◆

THE SAME THING HAPPENS if we begin from the opposite side and look on absorption, or entering, into the Self (whether by means of the Self's deliverance from all being that is conditioned by *I*, or by its being understood as the One thinking Essence) as the essential element in the religious act. By the first way of looking on the act it is imagined that God enters the being that is freed from *I*, or that this being is merged in God; by the second, that the being takes its stand directly in itself as though it were in the divine One. That is, by the first way, in a supreme moment the saying of the *Thou* ceases, for there is no more twofold being, and by the second the saying of the *Thou* does not in truth exist at all, for there is in truth no twofold being: the first way believes in the unification, the second in the identification of the human with the divine. Both assert a state that is beyond *I* and *Thou*, the first—as in ecstasy—one that becomes, the second—as in the self-observation of the thinking subject—one that is and that reveals itself. Both abolish relation, the first as it were dynamically, through the swallowing up of the *I* by the *Thou*—which is, however, no longer *Thou*, but that which alone is—and the second as it were statically through the self-recognition of the *I*, which has been freed and has become the Self, as that which alone is. If the doctrine of dependence considers the *I* that bears the span of pure relation in the world to be so weak and empty that its ability to bear it is no longer credible, the one doctrine of absorption causes the span of relation to disappear at its consummation, the other treats it as a delusion to be overcome.

The doctrines of absorption appeal to the great sayings of identification, the one above all to the Johannine "I and the Father are one," the other to the teaching of Sandilya: "The all-embracing, this is my Self in my very heart."

The ways these sayings lead are opposed to one another. The first arises (after a subterranean course) in the life of a person of mythical proportions and advances to a doctrine, the second emerges in a doctrine and only then leads to the mythical life of a person. The character of the saying is transformed along these lines. The Christ of the Johannine tradition, the Word that once became flesh, leads to the Christ of Eckhart, perpetually begotten by God in the human soul. The coronation formula for the Self in the Upanishad, "This is the real, the Self, and Thou art the Self," leads in a much shorter space to the Buddhistic formula of dethronement, "It is not possible to lay hold of a Self and a Self-appertaining in truth and in reality."

The beginning and end of each way demand separate consideration.

That the appeal to the ἐν ἔσμεν cannot be substantiated becomes clear to all who read impartially, section by section, the Gospel according to John. It is really the Gospel of pure relation. Here is a truer verse than the familiar mystical verse: "I am Thou and Thou art I." The Father and the Son, like in being—we may even say God and Man, like in being—are the indissolubly real pair, the two bearers of the primal relation, which from God to man is termed mission and command, from man to God looking and hearing, and between both is termed knowledge and love. In this relation the Son, though the Father dwells and works in him, bows down before the "greater" and prays to him. All modern attempts to interpret this primal reality of dialogue as a relation of the *I* to the Self, or the like—as an event that is contained within the self-sufficient interior life of man—are futile: they take their place in the abysmal history of destruction of reality.

—But what of mysticism? Does it not inform us how unity without duality is experienced? May we dispute the truth of its account?

—I know not of a single but of two kinds of happening in which duality is no longer experienced. These are at times confused in mystical utterances—I too once confused them.

The one is the soul's becoming a unity. That is something that

takes place not between man and God, but in man. Power is concentrated, everything that tries to divert it is drawn into the orbit
of its mastery, the being is alone in itself and rejoices, as Paracel-
sus says, in its exaltation. This is the decisive moment for a man.
Without it he is unfit for the work of the spirit; with it, he decides,
in his innermost being, if this means a breathing-space, or the sufficient end of his way. Concentrated in unity, he can go out to the
meeting, to which he has only now drawn quite close, with the
mystery, with salvation. But he can also enjoy to the full this
blessed concentration of his being, and without entering on the
supreme duty fall back into dissipation of being.—Everything on
our way involves decision, purposive, dimly seen, wholly mysterious: this in the innermost being is the primal mysterious decision, carrying the mightiest consequences for our destiny.

The other happening lies in the unfathomable nature of the
relational act itself, in which two, it is imagined, become one:
"one and one united, bareness shines there into bareness." *I* and
Thou are absorbed, humanity, which just before confronted the
godhead, is merged in it—glorification, deification, and singleness of being have appeared. But when the man, illuminated and
exhausted, falls back into the cares of earthly affairs, and with
knowledge in his heart thinks of the two situations, is he not
bound to find that his being is split asunder and one part given to
perdition? What does it help my soul that it can be withdrawn
anew from this world here into unity, when this world itself has of
necessity no part in the unity—what does all "enjoyment of God"
profit a life that is rent in two? If that abundantly rich heavenly
moment has nothing to do with my poor earthly moment—what
has it then to do with me, who have still to live, in all seriousness
still to live, on earth? Thus are the masters to be understood who
have renounced the raptures of ecstatic "union."

Union that was no union: as illustration I take the men who in
the passion of the engrossing Eros are so enraptured by the mira-
cle of the embrace that their knowledge of *I* and *Thou* perishes in

the feeling of a unity that does not and cannot exist. What the ecstatic man calls union is the enrapturing dynamic of relation, not a unity arisen in this moment of the world's time that dissolves the *I* and the *Thou*, but the dynamic of relation itself, which can put itself before its bearers as they steadily confront one another, and cover each from the feeling of the other enraptured one. Here, then, on the brink, the relational act goes beyond itself; the relation itself in its vital unity is felt so forcibly that its parts seem to fade before it, and in the force of *its* life, the *I* and the *Thou*, between which it is established, are forgotten. Here is one of the phenomena of the brink to which reality extends and at which it grows dim. But the central reality of the everyday hour on earth, with a streak of sun on a maple twig and the glimpse of the eternal *Thou*, is greater for us than all enigmatic webs on the brink of being.

This will, however, be opposed by the claim of the other doctrine of absorption that universal being and self-being are the same and that therefore no saying of the *Thou* is able to yield final reality.

This claim is answered by the doctrine itself. One of the Upanishads tells how Indra, the prince of the gods, comes to Prajapati, the creative spirit, in order to learn how the Self is found and recognised. For a hundred years he is a pupil, is twice dismissed with insufficient information, till finally the right information is given him: "If a man, sunk in deep sleep, rests dreamlessly, this is the Self, the Immortal, the Assured, the Universal Being." Indra departs, but soon a thought surprises him. He turns back and asks: "In such a condition, O Exalted One, a man does not know of his Self that 'This is I,' and that 'these are beings.' He is gone to annihilation. I see nothing propitious here."—"That," replies Prajapati, "is indeed so."

In so far as the doctrine contains an affirmation about true being—however the matter stands with its content of truth, which cannot be ascertained in this life—it has nothing in common with one thing, with lived reality; for it is bound to reduce this too to the world of appearances. In so far, too, as the doctrine contains guidance for absorption in true being, it leads not to lived reality but to "annihilation," where no consciousness reigns and whence no memory leads; the man who has emerged from this annihilation may still propose, as representing his experience, the limiting words "absence of duality"; he does not dare to call it unity.

But we with holy care wish to foster the holy good of our reality, that is gifted to us for this and perhaps for no other life that is nearer truth.

In lived reality there is no unity of being. Reality exists only in effective action, its power and depth in power and depth of effective action. "Inner" reality, too, exists only if there is mutual action. The most powerful and the deepest reality exists where everything enters into the effective action, without reserve the whole man and God the all-embracing—the united *I* and the boundless *Thou*.

The united *I:* for in lived reality there is (as I have already said) the becoming one of the soul, the concentration of power, the decisive moment for a man. But this does not involve, like that absorption, disregard of the real person. Absorption wishes to preserve only the "pure," the real, the lasting, and to cast away everything else; but in this concentration the instinctive is not thought too impure, the sensuous is not thought too remote from its course, what is concerned with emotion is not thought too fleeting: everything must be gathered into the orbit of its mastery. This concentration does not desire the self that is set apart, but the whole, unimpaired man. It aims at, and *is*, reality.

The doctrine of absorption demands, and promises, refuge in the One thinking Essence ("that by which this world is thought"), refuge in pure Subject. But in lived reality there is not something thinking without something thought, rather is the thinking no less dependent on the thing thought than the latter on the former. A subject deprived of its object is deprived of its reality. Something thinking in itself alone exists—in thought: first, as its product and object, as a limiting idea without an imaginable subject; secondly, by anticipation, in the definition of death, which can be replaced by its likeness of the deep sleep, which is just as impenetrable; and lastly, in the affirmation of the doctrine concerning a condition of absorption, resembling deep sleep, which is by nature without consciousness and memory. These are the loftiest peaks of the language of *It.* The sublime strength of their disregard must be respected, and in the very glance of respect recognised as what is, at most, to be experienced, but not to be lived.

The Buddha, the "fulfilled" and the fulfiller, makes no affirmation on this point. He refuses to assert that unity exists or that it does not exist, that he who has passed all the tests of absorption exists after death in unity or that he does not exist in unity. This refusal, this "noble silence," is explained in two ways: *one,* theoretical, because fulfilment is beyond the categories of thought and expression; and *two,* practical, because disclosure of the existence of fulfilment does not establish a true life of salvation. Combination of the two explanations indicates the truth that he who treats what is an object of assertion pulls it into division, into the antithetics of the world of *It,* where there *is* no life of salvation. "If, O monk, the opinion dominates that soul and body are one in being, there is no life of salvation; if, O monk, the opinion dominates that the soul is one and the body another, then too there is no life of salvation." In the mystery that is observed as in the reality that is lived, "It is thus" and "It is not thus," being and non-being, do not reign; but "thus and otherwise," being and non-being at once, the unfathomable—this reigns. The primal condition of salvation is undivided confrontation of the undivided mystery. It is certain that the Buddha is of those who have known this. Like all true teachers he does not wish to impart an opinion, but to teach the way. He denies only one assertion, that of the "fools," who say there is no action, no deed, no power, and says "Men can walk in the way." He ventures only one assertion, which is decisive: "There is, O Monks, an Unborn, neither become nor created nor formed." If there were not this, there would be no goal; there is this, the way has a goal.

Loyal to the truth of our meeting, we can follow the Buddha as far as this, but a step further would be disloyalty to the reality of our life.

For we know, from the truth and reality that we do not extract from ourselves but which is given for us to share in, that if the goal described by the Buddha is only one of the goals, then it cannot be ours, and if it is *the* goal, then it is falsely described; and also, if it is one of the goals, the way may lead as far as it, and if it is *the* goal, the way leads, at most, nearer to it.

The Buddha describes as the goal the "cessation of pain," that is of becoming and passing away—release from the cycle of births. "Henceforth there is no return" is the formula of the man who has freed himself from the appetite for living and thus from the necessity to become ever anew. We do not know if there is a return; we do not extend beyond this life the lines of this time-dimension in which we live, and do not seek to expose what will be disclosed to us in its own time and disposition. But if we did know that there is a return we would not seek to escape it, and we would long not indeed for gross being but for the power to speak, in each existence in its own way and language, the eternal *I* that passes away, and the eternal *Thou* that does not pass away.

We do not know if the Buddha actually leads to the goal of release from the necessity of returning. He certainly leads to a preliminary goal that concerns us—to the becoming one of the soul. But he leads thither not merely (as is necessary) apart from the "thicket of opinions," but also apart from the "illusion of forms"—which for us is no illusion but rather the reliable world (and this in spite of all subjective paradoxes in observation *connected with it for us*). His way, too, then, involves disregard; thus when he speaks of our becoming aware of the events in our body he means almost the opposite of our physical insight with its certainty about the senses. Nor does he lead the united being further to that supreme saying of the *Thou* that is made possible for it. His innermost decision seems to rest on the extinction of the ability to say *Thou.*

The Buddha knows the saying of the *Thou* to men—witness his intercourse with his pupils, in which, though high above them, he speaks very directly—but he does not teach it; for simple confrontation of being with being is alien to this love where "all that has become is illimitably comprised in the breast." He certainly knows too, in the silent depths of his being, the saying of the *Thou* to the primal cause—away beyond all those "gods" that are treated by him like pupils. This act of his springs from a relational event that has taken on substance; this act, too, is a response to the *Thou:* but about this response he preserves silence.

His succession among the peoples, however, that "great vehicle," has contradicted him magnificently. It has addressed the eternal human *Thou* under the name of Buddha himself. And it awaits, as the Buddha that is to come, the last of the age, him by whom love is to be fulfilled.

All doctrine of absorption is based on the colossal illusion of the human spirit that is bent back on itself, that spirit exists in man. Actually spirit exists with man as starting-point—between man and that which is not man. In renouncing this its meaning, its meaning as relation, the spirit that is bent back on itself is compelled to drag into man that which is not man, it is compelled to make the world and God into functions of the soul. This is the spirit's illusion about the soul.

"Friend," says the Buddha, "I proclaim that in this my fathom-high ascetic's body, affected with sensations, there dwells the world and the beginning of the world and the extinction of the world and the way that leads to the extinction of the world."

That is true, but in the last resort it is no longer true.

Certainly the world "dwells" in me as an image, just as I dwell in it as a thing. But it is not for that reason in me, just as I am not in it. The world and I are mutually included, the one in the other. This contradiction in thought, inherent in the situation of *It,* is resolved in the situation of *Thou,* which sets me free from the world in order to bind me up in solidarity of connexion with it.

I bear within me the sense of Self, that cannot be included in the world. The world bears within itself the sense of being, that cannot be included in the image. This sense of being, however, is not a "will" that can be thought, but simply the total status of the world as world, just as the sense of Self is not a "knowing subject" but simply the total status of the *I* as *I.* Here no further "reduction" is possible; he who does not honour the last unities frustrates their apprehensible but not comprehensible sense.

The beginning and the extinction of the world are not in me; but they are also not outside me; they cannot be said to *be* at all, they are a continuous happening, connected with and dependent on me, my life, my decision, my work, and my service. But they do depend not on whether I "affirm" or "deny" the world in my soul, but on how I cause my attitude of soul to the world to grow to life, to life that acts upon the world, to real life—and in real life the ways of very different attitudes of soul may intersect. But he who merely "experiences" his attitude, merely consummates it in the soul, however thoughtfully, is without the world—and all the tricks, arts, ecstasies, enthusiasms, and mysteries that are in him do not even ripple the skin of the world. So long as a man is set free only in his Self he can do the world neither weal nor woe; he does not concern the world. Only he who believes in the world is given power to enter into dealings with it, and if he gives himself to this he cannot remain godless. If only we love the real world, that will not let itself be extinguished, really in its horror, if only we venture to surround it with the arms of our spirit, our hands will meet the hands which held it fast.

I know nothing of a "world" and a "life in the world" that might separate a man from God. What is thus described is actually life with an alienated world of *It,* which experiences and uses. He who truly goes out to meet the world goes out also to God. Concentration and outgoing are necessary, both in truth, at once the one and the other, which is the One.

God comprises, but is not, the universe. So, too, God comprises, but is not, my Self. In view of the inadequacy of any language about this fact, I can say *Thou* in my language as each man can in his, in view of this *I* and *Thou* live, and dialogue and spirit and language (spirit's primal act), and the Word in eternity.

◆

MAN'S RELIGIOUS SITUATION, his *being there* in the Presence, is characterised by its essential and indissoluble antinomy. The nature of its being determines that this antinomy is indissoluble. He who accepts the thesis and rejects the antithesis does injury to the significance of the situation. He who tries to think out a synthesis destroys the significance of the situation. He who strives to make the antinomy into a relative matter abolishes the significance of the situation. He who wishes to carry through the conflict of the antinomy other than with his life transgresses the significance of the situation. The significance of the situation is that it is lived, and nothing but lived, continually, ever anew, without foresight, without forethought, without prescription, in the totality of its antinomy.

Comparison of the religious with the philosophical antinomy will make this clear. Kant may make the philosophical conflict between necessity and freedom into a relative matter by assigning the former to the world of appearances and the latter to the world of being, so that in their two settings they are no longer really opposed, but rather reconciled—just as the worlds for which they are valid are reconciled. But if I consider necessity and freedom not in worlds of thought but in the reality of my standing before God, if I know that "I am given over for disposal" and know at the same time that "It depends on myself," then I cannot try to escape the paradox that has to be lived by assigning the irreconcilable propositions to two separate realms of validity; nor can I be helped to an ideal reconciliation by any theological device: but I am compelled to take both to myself, to be lived together, and in being lived they are one.

✦

AN ANIMAL'S EYES have the power to speak a great language. Independently, without needing co-operation of sounds and gestures, most forcibly when they rely wholly on their glance, the eyes express the mystery in its natural prison, the anxiety of becoming. This condition of the mystery is known only by the animal, it alone can disclose it to us—and this condition only lets itself be disclosed, not fully revealed. The language in which it is uttered is what it says—anxiety, the movement of the creature between the realms of vegetable security and spiritual venture. This language is the stammering of nature at the first touch of spirit, before it yields to spirit's cosmic venture that we call man. But no speech will ever repeat what that stammering knows and can proclaim.

Sometimes I look into a cat's eyes. The domesticated animal has not as it were received from us (as we sometimes imagine) the gift of the truly "speaking" glance, but only—at the price of its primitive disinterestedness—the capacity to turn its glance to us prodigious beings. But with this capacity there enters the glance, in its dawn and continuing in its rising, a quality of amazement and of inquiry that is wholly lacking in the original glance with all its anxiety. The beginning of this cat's glance, lighting up under the touch of my glance, indisputably questioned me: "It is possible that you think of me? Do you really not just want me to have fun? Do I concern you? Do I exist in your sight? Do I really exist? What is it that comes from you? What is it that surrounds me? What is it that comes to me? What is it?" ("I" is here a transcription for a word, that we do not have, denoting self without the ego; and by "it" is to be imagined the streaming human glance in the total reality of its power to enter into relation.) The animal's glance, speech of disquietude, rose in its greatness—and set at once. My own glance was certainly more lasting; but it was no longer the streaming human glance.

The rotation of the world which introduced the relational event had been followed almost immediately by the other which ended it. The world of *It* surrounded the animal and myself, for the space of a glance the world of *Thou* had shone out from the depths, to be at once extinguished and put back into the world of *It*.

I relate this tiny episode, which I have experienced several times, for the sake of the speech of this almost unnoticeable sunrise and sunset of the spirit. In no other speech have I known so profoundly the fleeting nature of actuality in all its relations with being, the exalted melancholy of our fate, the change, heavy with destiny, of every isolated *Thou* into an *It*. For other events possessed between morning and evening their day, even though it might be brief; but here morning and evening flowed pitilessly mingled together, the bright *Thou* appeared and was gone. Had the burden of the world of *It* really been removed for the space of a glance from the animal and from myself? I myself could continue to think about the matter, but the animal had sunk back out of the stammer of its glance into the disquietude where there is no speech and almost no memory.

How powerful is the unbroken world of *It*, and how delicate are the appearances of the *Thou*!

So much can never break through the crust of the condition of things! O fragment of mica, looking on which I once learned, for the first time, that *I* is not something "in me"—with you I was nevertheless only bound up in myself; at that time the event took place only in me, not between me and you. But when one that is alive rises out of things, and becomes a being in relation to me, joined to me by its nearness and its speech, for how inevitably short a time is it nothing to me but *Thou*! It is not the relation that necessarily grows feeble, but the actuality of its immediacy. Love itself cannot persist in the immediacy of relation; love endures, but in the interchange of actual and potential being. Every *Thou* in the world is enjoined by its nature to become a thing for us, or at all events to re-enter continually the condition of things.

Only in one, all-embracing relation is potential still actual being. Only one *Thou* never ceases by its nature to be *Thou* for us. He who knows God knows also very well remoteness from God, and the anguish of barrenness in the tormented heart; but he does not know the absence of God: it is we only who are not always there.

The lover in the *Vita Nuova* rightly and properly says for the most part *Ella* and only at times *Voi*. The spectator of the *Paradiso*, when he says *Colui*, speaks from poetic necessity, and knows it. If God is addressed as He or It, it is always allegorically. But if we say *Thou* to Him, then mortal sense has set the unbroken truth of the world into a word.

◆

EVERY REAL RELATION in the world is exclusive, the Other breaks in on it and avenges its exclusion. Only in the relation with God are unconditioned exclusiveness and unconditioned inclusiveness one and the same, in which the whole universe is implied.

Every real relation in the world rests on individuation, this is its joy—for only in this way is mutual knowledge of different beings won—and its limitation—for in this way perfect knowledge and being known are foregone. But in the perfect relation my *Thou* comprehends but is not my Self, my limited knowledge opens out into a state in which I am boundlessly known.

Every real relation in the world is consummated in the interchange of actual and potential being; every isolated *Thou* is bound to enter the chrysalis state of the *It* in order to take wings anew. But in pure relation potential being is simply actual being as it draws breath, and in it the *Thou* remains present. By its nature the eternal *Thou* is eternally *Thou;* only our nature compels us to draw it into the world and the talk of *It*.

◆

THE WORLD OF *It* is set in the context of space and time.

The world of *Thou* is not set in the context of either of these.

Its context is in the Centre, where the extended lines of relations meet—in the eternal *Thou*.

In the great privilege of pure relation the privileges of the world of *It* are abolished. By virtue of this privilege there exists the unbroken world of *Thou:* the isolated moments of relations are bound up in a life of world solidarity. By virtue of this privilege formative power belongs to the world of *Thou:* spirit can penetrate and transform the world of *It*. By virtue of this privilege we are not given up to alienation from the world and the loss of reality by the *I*—to domination by the ghostly. Turning is the recognition of the Centre and the act of turning again to it. In this act of the being the buried relational power of man rises again, the wave that carries all the spheres of relation swells in living streams to give new life to our world.

Perhaps not to our world alone. For this double movement, of estrangement from the primal Source, in virtue of which the universe is sustained in the process of becoming, and of turning towards the primal Source, in virtue of which the universe is released in being, may be perceived as the metacosmical primal form that dwells in the world as a whole in its relation to that which is not the world—form whose twofold nature is represented among men by the twofold nature of their attitudes, their primary words, and their aspects of the world. Both parts of this movement develop, fraught with destiny, in time, and are compassed by grace in the timeless creation that is, incomprehensibly, at once emancipation and preservation, release and binding. Our knowledge of twofold nature is silent before the paradox of the primal mystery.

◆

THE SPHERES IN WHICH THE WORLD OF RELATION is built are three.

First, our life with nature, in which the relation clings to the threshold of speech.

Second, our life with men, in which the relation takes on the form of speech.

Third, our life with spiritual beings, where the relation, being without speech, yet begets it.

In every sphere in its own way, through each process of becoming that is present to us, we look out toward the fringe of the eternal *Thou;* in each we are aware of a breath from the eternal *Thou;* in each *Thou* we address the eternal *Thou.*

Every sphere is compassed in the eternal *Thou,* but it is not compassed in them.

Through every sphere shines the one present.

We can, however, remove each sphere from the present.

From our life with nature we can lift out the "physical" world, the world of consistency, from our life with men the "psychical" world, the world of sensibility, and from our life with spiritual beings the "noetic" world, the world of validity. But now their transparency, and with it their meaning, has been taken from them; each sphere has become dull and capable of being used— and remains dull even though we light it up with the names of Cosmos and Eros and Logos. For actually there is a cosmos for man only when the universe becomes his home, with its holy hearth whereon he offers sacrifice; there is Eros for man only when beings become for him pictures of the eternal, and community is revealed along with them; and there is Logos for man only when he addresses the mystery with work and service for the spirit.

Form's silent asking, man's loving speech, the mute proclamation of the creature, are all gates leading into the presence of the Word.

But when the full and complete meeting is to take place, the gates are united in one gateway of real life, and you no longer know through which you have entered.

✦

OF THE THREE SPHERES, one, our life with men, is marked out. Here language is consummated as a sequence, in speech and counter-speech. Here alone does the word that is formed in language meet its response. Only here does the primary word go backwards and forwards in the same form, the word of address and the word of response live in the one language, *I* and *Thou* take their stand not merely in relation, but also in the solid give-and-take of talk. The moments of relation are here, and only here, bound together by means of the element of the speech in which they are immersed. Here what confronts us has blossomed into the full reality of the *Thou*. Here alone, then, as reality that cannot be lost, are gazing and being gazed upon, knowing and being known, loving and being loved.

This is the main portal, into whose opening the two side-gates lead, and in which they are included.

"When a man is together with his wife the longing of the eternal hills blows round about them."

The relation with man is the real simile of the relation with God; in it true address receives true response; except that in God's response everything, the universe, is made manifest as language.

✦

—BUT IS NOT SOLITUDE, TOO, A GATE? Is there not at times disclosed, in stillest loneliness, an unsuspected perception? Can concern with oneself not mysteriously be transformed into concern with the mystery? Indeed, is not that man alone who no longer adheres to any being worthy to confront the Being? "Come, lonely One, to him who is alone," cries Simeon, the new theologian, to his God.

—There are two kinds of solitude, according to that from which they have turned. If we call it solitude to free oneself from intercourse of experiencing and using of things, then that is always necessary, in order that the act of relation, and not that of the supreme relation only, may be reached. But if solitude means absence of relation, then he who has been forsaken by the beings to which he spoke the true *Thou* will be raised up by God, but not he who himself forsook the beings. He alone adheres to various ones of these who is greedy to use them; but he who lives in the strength of present realisation can only be bound up in relation with them. And he alone who is so bound is ready for God. For he alone confronts the reality of God with a human reality.

Further, there are two kinds of solitude, according to that towards which they have turned. If solitude is the place of purification, necessary even to the man who is bound in relation, both before he enters the Holy of Holies and in the midst of his ventures between unavoidable failing and the ascent to proving true—to this solitude we are by nature disposed. But if solitude is the stronghold of isolation, where a man conducts a dialogue with himself—not in order to test and master himself for that which awaits him but in the enjoyment of the conformation of his soul—then we have the real fall of the spirit into spirituality. The man can advance to the last abyss, where in his self-delusion he imagines he has God to himself and is speaking with Him. But truly though God surrounds us and dwells in us, we never have Him in us. And we speak with Him only when speech dies within us.

◆

A MODERN PHILOSOPHER supposes that every man necessarily believes either in God or in "idols," that is, in some sort of finite good—his nation, his art, power, knowledge, the amassing of money, "the ever new subjugation of woman"—which has become for him an absolute value and has set itself up between him and God; it is only necessary to demonstrate to him the conditioned nature of this good, in order to "shatter" the idol, and the diverted religious act will automatically return to the fitting object.

This conception presupposes that man's relation to the finite goods he has "idolized" is of the same nature as his relation to God, and differs only in its object; for only with this presupposition could the mere substitution of the true for the false object save the erring man. But a man's relation to the "special something" that usurps the throne of the supreme value of his life, and supplants eternity, rests always on experiencing and using an *It*, a thing, an object of enjoyment. For this relation alone is able to obstruct the prospect which opens towards God—it is the impenetrable world of *It;* but the relation which involves the saying of the *Thou* opens up this prospect ever anew. He who is dominated by the idol that he wishes to win, to hold, and to keep—possessed by a desire for possession—has no way to God but that of turning, which is a change not only of goal but also of the nature of his movement. The man who is possessed is saved by being wakened and educated to solidarity of relation, not by being led in his state of possession towards God. If a man remains in this state what does it mean when he calls no longer on the name of a demon or of a being demonically distorted for him, but on the name of God? It means that from now on he blasphemes. It is blasphemy when a man wishes, after the idol has crashed behind the altar, to pile up an unholy sacrifice to God on the desecrated place.

He who loves a woman, and brings her life to present realisation in his, is able to look in the *Thou* of her eyes into a beam of the eternal *Thou*. But he who eagerly desires "ever new subjugation"—do you wish to hold out to his desire a phantom of the Eternal? He who serves his people in the boundlessness of destiny, and is willing to give himself to them, is really thinking of God. But do you suppose that the man to whom the nation is a god, in whose service he would like to enlist everything (for in the nation's he exalts his own image), need only be given a feeling of disgust—and he would see the truth? And what does it mean that a man is said to treat money, embodied non-being, "as if it were God"? What has the lust of grabbing and of laying up treasure in common with the joy in the presence of the Present One? Can the servant of Mammon say *Thou* to his money? And how is he to behave towards God when he does not understand how to say *Thou*? He cannot serve two masters—not even one after the other: he must first learn to serve *in a different way.*

He who has been converted by this substitution of object now "holds" a phantom that he calls God. But God, the eternal Presence, does not permit Himself to be held. Woe to the man so possessed that he thinks he possesses God!

◆

THE "RELIGIOUS" MAN is spoken of as one who does not need to take his stand in any relation to the world and to living beings, since the status of social life, that is defined from outside, is in him surpassed by means of a strength that works only from within. But in this idea of the social life two basically different things are combined—first, the community that is built up out of relation, and second, the collection of human units that do not know relation—modern man's palpable condition of lack of relation. But the bright building of community, to which there is an escape even from the dungeon of "social life," is the achievement of the same power that works in the relation between man and God. This does not mean that this one relation is set beside the others; for it is the universal relation, into which all streams pour, yet without exhausting their waters. Who wishes to make division and define boundaries between sea and streams? There we find only the one flow from *I* to *Thou,* unending, the one boundless flow of the real life. Life cannot be divided between a real relation with God and an unreal relation of *I* and *It* with the world—you cannot both truly pray to God and profit by the world. He who knows the world as something by which he is to profit knows God also in the same way. His prayer is a procedure of exoneration heard by the ear of the void. He—not the "atheist," who addresses the Nameless out of the night and yearning of his garret-window—is the godless man.

It is further said that the "religious" man stands as a single, isolated, separated being before God, since he has also gone beyond the status of the "moral" man, who is still involved in duty and obligation to the world. The latter, it is said, is still burdened with responsibility for the action of those who act, since he is wholly defined by the tension between being and "ought to be," and in grotesque and hopeless sacrificial courage casts his heart piece by piece into the insatiable gulf that lies between them. The "religious" man, on the other hand, has emerged from that tension into the tension between the world and God; there the command reigns that the unrest of responsibility and of demands on oneself be removed; there is no willing of one's own, but only the being joined into what is ordained; every "ought" vanishes in unconditioned being, and the world, though still existing, no longer counts. For in it the "religious" man has to perform his particular duties, but as it were without obligation—beneath the aspect of the nothingness of all action. But that is to suppose that God has created His world as an illusion and man for frenzied being. He who approaches the Face has indeed surpassed duty and obligation—but not because he is now remote from the world; rather because he has truly drawn closer to it. Duty and obligation are rendered only to the stranger; we are drawn to and full of love for the intimate person. The world, lit by eternity, becomes fully present to him who approaches the Face, and to the Being of beings he can in a single response say *Thou*. Then there is no more tension between the world and God, but only the one reality. The man is not freed from responsibility; he has exchanged the torment of the finite, pursuit of effects, for the motive power of the infinite, he has got the mighty responsibility of love for the whole untraceable world-event, for the profound belonging to the world before the Face of God. He has, to be sure, abolished moral judgments for ever; the "evil" man is simply one who is commended to him for greater responsibility, one more needy of love; but he will have to practise, till death itself, decision in the depths of spontaneity, unruffled decision, made ever anew, to right action. Then action is not empty, but purposive, enjoined, needed, part of creation; but this action is no longer imposed upon the world, it grows on it as if it were non-action.

◆

WHAT IS THE ETERNAL, primal phenomenon, present here and now, of that which we term revelation? It is the phenomenon that a man does not pass, from the moment of the supreme meeting, the same being as he entered into it. The moment of meeting is not an "experience" that stirs in the receptive soul and grows to perfect blessedness; rather, in that moment something happens to the man. At times it is like a light breath, at times like a wrestling-bout, but always—it *happens*. The man who emerges from the act of pure relation that so involves his being has now in his being something more that has grown in him, of which he did not know before and whose origin he is not rightly able to indicate. However the source of this new thing is classified in scientific orientation of the world, with its authorised efforts to establish an unbroken causality, we, whose concern is real consideration of the real, cannot have our purpose served with subconsciousness or any other apparatus of the soul. The reality is that we receive what we did not hitherto have, and receive it in such a way that we know it has been given to us. In the language of the Bible, "Those who wait upon the Lord shall renew their strength." In the language of Nietzsche, who in his account remains loyal to reality, "We take and do not ask who it is there that gives."

Man receives, and he receives not a specific "content" but a Presence, a Presence as power. This Presence and this power include three things, undivided, yet in such a way that we may consider them separately. First, there is the whole fulness of real mutual action, of the being raised and bound up in relation: the man can give no account at all of how the binding in relation is brought about, nor does it in any way lighten his life—it makes life heavier, but heavy with meaning. Secondly, there is the inexpressible confirmation of meaning. Meaning is assured. Nothing can any longer be meaningless. The question about the meaning of life is no longer there. But were it there, it would not have to be answered. You do not know how to exhibit and define the meaning of life, you have no formula or picture for it, and yet it has more certitude for you than the perceptions of your senses. What does the revealed and concealed meaning purpose with us, desire from us? It does not wish to be explained (nor are we able to do that) but only to be done by us. Thirdly, this meaning is not that of "another life," but that of this life of ours, not one of a world "yonder" but that of this world of ours, and it desires its confirmation in this life and in relation with this world. This meaning can be received, but not experienced; it cannot be experienced but it can be done, and this is its purpose with us. The assurance I have of it does not wish to be sealed within me, but it wishes to be born by me into the world. But just as the meaning itself does not permit itself to be transmitted and made into knowledge generally current and admissible, so confirmation of it cannot be transmitted as a valid Ought; it is not prescribed, it is not specified on any tablet, to be raised above all men's heads. The meaning that has been received can be proved true by each man only in the singleness of his being and the singleness of his life. As no prescription can lead us to the meeting, so none leads from it. As only acceptance of the Presence is necessary for the approach to the meeting, so in a new sense is it so when we emerge from it. As we reach the meeting with the simple *Thou* on our lips, so with the *Thou* on our lips we leave it and return to the world.

That before which, in which, out of which, and into which we live, even the mystery, has remained what it was. It has become present to us and in its presentness has proclaimed itself to us as salvation; we have "known" it, but we acquire no knowledge from it which might lessen or moderate its mysteriousness. We have come near to God, but not nearer to unveiling being or solving its riddle. We have felt release, but not discovered a "solution." We cannot approach others with what we have received, and say "You must know this, you must do this." We can only go, and confirm its truth. And this, too, is no "ought," but we can, we *must*.

This is the eternal revelation that is present here and now. I know of no revelation and believe in none whose primal phenomenon is not precisely this. I do not believe in a self-naming of God; a self-definition of God before men. The Word of revelation is *I am that I am.* That which reveals is that which reveals. That which is *is,* and nothing more. The eternal source of strength streams, the eternal contact persists, the eternal voice sounds forth, and nothing more.

◆

THE ETERNAL *Thou* can by its nature not become *It;* for by its nature it cannot be established in measure and bounds, not even in the measure of the immeasurable, or the bounds of boundless being; for by its nature it cannot be understood as a sum of qualities, not even as an infinite sum of qualities raised to a transcendental level; for it can be found neither in nor out of the world; for it cannot be experienced, or thought; for we miss Him, Him who is, if we say "I believe, that He is"—"He" is also a metaphor, but "Thou" is not.

And yet in accordance with our nature we are continually making the eternal *Thou* into *It,* into some thing—making God into a thing. Not indeed out of arbitrary self-will; God's history as a thing, the passage of God as Thing through religion and through the products on its brink, through its bright ways and its gloom, its enhancement and its destruction of life, the passage away from the living God and back again to Him, the changes from the present to establishment of form, of objects, and of ideas, dissolution and renewal—all are one way, are *the* way.

What is the origin of the expressed knowledge and ordered action of the religions? How do the Presence and the power of the revelation (for all religions necessarily appeal to some kind of revelation, whether through the medium of the spoken word, or of nature, or of the soul: there are only religions of revelation)—how do the Presence and the power received by men in revelation change into a "content"?

The explanation has two layers. We understand the outer psychical layer when we consider man in himself, separated from history, and the inner factual layer, the primal phenomenon of religion, when we replace him in history. The two layers belong together.

Man desires to possess God; he desires a continuity in space and time of possession of God. He is not content with the inexpressible confirmation of meaning, but wants to see this confirmation stretched out as something that can be continually taken up and handled, a continuum unbroken in space and time that insures his life at every point and every moment.

Man's thirst for continuity is unsatisfied by the life-rhythm of pure relation, the interchange of actual being and of a potential being in which only our power to enter into relation, and hence the presentness (but not the primal Presence) decreases. He longs for extension in time, for duration. Thus God becomes an object of faith. At first faith, set in time, completes the acts of relation; but gradually it replaces them. Resting in belief in an *It* takes the place of the continually renewed movement of the being towards concentration and going out to the relation. The "Nevertheless I believe" of the fighter who knows remoteness from as well as nearness to God is more and more completely transformed into the certainty of him who enjoys profits, that nothing can happen to him, since he believes that there is One who will not let anything happen to him.

Further, man's thirst for continuity is unsatisfied by the life-structure of pure relation, the "solitude" of the *I* before the *Thou*, the law that man, though binding up the world in relation in the meeting, can nevertheless only as a person approach and meet God. He longs for extension in space, for the representation in which the community of the faithful is united with its God. Thus God becomes the object of a cult. The cult, too, completes at first the acts of relation, in adjusting in a spatial context of great forma-tive power the living prayer, the immediate saying of the *Thou*, and in linking it with the life of the senses. It, too, gradually replaces the acts of relation, when the personal prayer is no longer supported, but displaced, by the communal prayer, and when the act of the being, since it admits no rule, is replaced by ordered devotional exercises.

Actually, however, pure relation can only be raised to con-stancy in space and time by being embodied in the whole stuff of life. It cannot be preserved, but only proved true, only done, only done up into life. Man can do justice to the relation with God in which he has come to share only if he realises God anew in the world according to his strength and to the measure of each day. In this lies the only authentic assurance of continuity. The authentic assurance of duration consists in the fact that pure relation can be fulfilled in the growth and rise of beings into *Thou*, that the holy primary word makes itself heard in them all. Thus the time of human life is shaped into a fulness of reality, and even though human life neither can nor ought to overcome the connexion with *It*, it is so penetrated with relation that relation wins in it a shin-ing streaming constancy: the moments of supreme meeting are then not flashes in darkness but like the rising moon in a clear starlit night. Thus, too, the authentic assurance of constancy in space consists in the fact that men's relations with their true *Thou*, the radial lines that proceed from all the points of the *I* to the Centre, form a circle. It is not the periphery, the community, that comes first, but the radii, the common quality of relation with the Centre. This alone guarantees the authentic existence of the community.

Only when these two arise—the binding up of time in a relational life of salvation and the binding up of space in the community that is made one by its Centre—and only so long as they exist, does there arise and exist, round about the invisible altar, a human cosmos with bounds and form, grasped with the spirit out of the universal stuff of the æon, a world that is house and home, a dwelling for man in the universe.

Meeting with God does not come to man in order that he may concern himself with God, but in order that he may confirm that there is meaning in the world. All revelation is summons and sending. But again and again man brings about, instead of realisation, a reflexion to Him who reveals: he wishes to concern himself with God instead of with the world. Only, in such a reflexion, he is no longer confronted by a *Thou,* he can do nothing but establish an It–God in the realm of things, believe that he knows of God as of an *It,* and so speak about Him. Just as the "self"-seeking man, instead of directly living something or other, a perception or an affection, reflects about his perspective or reflective *I,* and thereby misses the truth of the event, so the man who seeks God (though for the rest he gets on very well with the self-seeker in the one soul), instead of allowing the gift to work itself out, reflects about the Giver—and misses both.

God remains present to you when you have been sent forth; he who goes on a mission has always God before him: the truer the fulfilment the stronger and more constant His nearness. To be sure, he cannot directly concern himself with God, but he can converse with Him. Reflexion, on the other hand, makes God into an object. Its apparent turning towards the primal source belongs in truth to the universal movement away from it; just as the apparent turning away of the man who is fulfilling his mission belongs in truth to the universal movement towards the primal source.

For the two primary metacosmical movements of the world—

expansion into its own being and turning to connexion—find their supreme human form, the real spiritual form of their struggle and adjustment, their mingling and separation, in the history of the human relation to God. In turning the Word is born on earth, in expansion the Word enters the chrysalis form of religion, in fresh turning it is born again with new wings.

Arbitrary self-will does not reign here, even though the movement towards the *It* goes at times so far that it threatens to suppress and to smother the movement out again to the *Thou*.

The mighty revelations to which the religions appeal are like in being with the quiet revelations that are to be found everywhere and at all times. The mighty revelations which stand at the beginning of great communities and at the turning-point of an age are nothing but the eternal revelation. But the revelation does not pour itself into the world through him who receives it as through a funnel; it comes to him and seizes his whole elemental being in all its particular nature, and fuses with it. The man, too, who is the "mouth" of the revelation, is indeed this, not a speaking-tube or any kind of instrument, but an organ, which sounds according to its own laws; and to sound means to *modify*.

The various ages of history, however, show a qualitative difference. There is a time of maturing, when the true element of the human spirit, suppressed and buried, comes to hidden readiness so urgent and so tense that it awaits only a touch from Him who touches in order to burst forth. The revelation that then makes its appearance seizes in the totality of its constitution the whole elemental stuff that is thus prepared, melts it down, and produces in it a form that is a new form of God in the world.

Thus in the course of history, in the transforming of elemental human stuff, ever new provinces of the world and the spirit are raised to form, summoned to divine form. Ever new spheres become regions of a theophany. It is not man's own power that works here, nor is it God's pure effective passage, but it is a mixture of the divine and the human. He who is sent out in the strength of revelation takes with him, in his eyes, an image of God; however far this exceeds the senses, yet he takes it with him in the eye of the spirit, in that visual power of his spirit which is not metaphorical but wholly real. The spirit responds also through a look, a look that is *formative*. Although we earthly beings never look at God without the world, but only look at the world in God, yet as we look we shape eternally the form of God.

Form is also a mixture of *Thou* and *It*. In belief and in a cult form can harden into an object; but, in virtue of the essential quality of relation that lives on in it, it continually becomes present again. God is near His forms so long as man does not remove them from Him. In true prayer belief and cult are united and purified to enter into the living relation. The fact that true prayer lives in the religions witnesses to their true life: they live so long as it lives in them. Degeneration of the religions means degeneration of prayer in them. Their power to enter into relation is buried under increasing objectification, it becomes increasingly difficult for them to say *Thou* with the whole undivided being, and finally, in order to be able to say it, man must come out of the false security into the venture of the infinite—out of the community, that is now over-arched only by the temple dome and not also by the firmament, into the final solitude. It is a profound misunderstanding of this impulse to ascribe it to "subjectivism"; life face to face with God is life in the one reality, the only true "objective," and the man who goes out to this life desires to save himself, in the objective that truly *is*, from that which is apparent and illusory, before it has disturbed the truth of the real objective for him. Subjectivism empties God of soul, objectivism makes Him into an object—the latter is a false fixing down, the former a false setting free; both are diversions from the way of reality, both are attempts to replace reality.

God is near His forms if man does not remove them from Him. But when the expanding movement of religion suppresses the movement of turning and removes the form from God, the countenance of the form is obliterated, its lips are dead, its hands hang down, God knows it no more, and the universal dwelling-place that is built about its altar, the spiritually apprehended cosmos, tumbles in. And the fact that man, in the disturbance of his truth, no longer sees what is then taking place, is a part of what has then taken place.

Disintegration of the Word has taken place.

The Word has its essence in revelation, its effect in the life of the form, its currency during the domination of the form that has died.

This is the course and the counter-course of the eternal and eternally present Word in history.

The times in which the living Word appears are those in which the solidarity of connexion between *I* and the world is renewed; the times in which the effective Word reigns are those in which the agreement between *I* and the world are maintained; the times in which the Word becomes current are those in which alienation between *I* and the world, loss of reality, growth of fate, is completed—till there comes the great shudder, the holding of the breath in the dark, and the preparing silence.

But this course is not circular. It is the way. In each new æon fate becomes more oppressive, turning more shattering. And the theophany becomes ever *nearer,* increasingly near to the sphere that lies *between beings,* to the Kingdom that is hidden in our midst, there between us. History is a mysterious approach. Every spiral of its way leads us both into profounder perversion and more fundamental turning. But the event that from the side of the world is called turning is called from God's side redemption.

Postscript

1

WHEN I DRAFTED THE FIRST SKETCH of this book (more than forty years ago), I was impelled by an inward necessity. A vision which had come to me again and again since my youth, and which had been clouded over again and again, had now reached steady clarity. This clarity was so manifestly suprapersonal in its nature that I at once knew I had to bear witness to it. Some time after I had received the right word as well, and could write the book again in its final form,[1] it became apparent that while there was need of some additions these had to be in their own place and in independent form. In this way there arose some shorter writings,[2] which clarified the vision by means of examples, or explained it in face of objections, or criticised views to which it indeed owed important points but upon which my most essential concern had not dawned in its central significance—namely, the close connexion of the relation to God with the relation to one's fellow-man. Later there were added some references to anthropological foundations[3] and to

---

[1] It appeared in German in 1923, in English in 1937.

[2] *Zwiesprache,* 1932; *Die Frage an den Einzelnen,* 1938; *Rede über das Erzieherische,* 1926; *Das Problem des Menschen,* first edition in Hebrew, 1942, German in the volume *Dialogisches Leben,* 1947, individual edition, 1948. English editions appeared in one volume, *Between Man and Man,* 1947.

[3] *Urdistanz und Beziehung,* 1951, "Distance and Relation," *Psychiatry,* Vol. XX, No. 2 (May 1957), pp. 97–104. To be included in Martin Buber, *We: Studies in Philosophical Anthropology.*

sociological consequences.[1] Nevertheless it has turned out that by no means everything has been sufficiently clarified. Again and again readers have turned to me to ask about the meaning of this and that. For a long time I answered each individually, but I gradually realised that I was not able to do justice to the demand laid upon me; besides, I must not limit the dialogical relationship to those readers who make up their minds to speak: perhaps there are many among the silent who deserve special consideration. So I have had to set about giving a public answer, first of all to some essential questions which are bound together by their meaning.

2

The first question may be formulated with some precision as follows: If—as the book says—we can stand in the *I–Thou* relationship not merely with other men, but also with beings and things which come to meet us in nature, what is it that makes the real difference between the two relationships? Or, more closely, if the *I–Thou* relationship requires a mutual action which in fact embraces both the *I* and the *Thou,* how may the relation to something in nature be understood as such a relationship? More precisely still, if we are to assume that we are granted a kind of mutuality by beings and things in nature as well, which we meet as our *Thou,* what is then the character of this reciprocity and what justification have we for using this fundamental concept in order to describe it?

Clearly there is no unified answer to this question. Instead of

[1]"Elemente des Zwischenmenschlichen," in the volume *Die Schriften über das dialogische Prinzip,* 1954, "Elements of the Interhuman," *Psychiatry,* Vol. XX, No. 2 (May 1937), pp. 103–113. To be included in Martin Buber, *We: Studies in Philosophical Anthropology.*

grasping nature as a whole, in our customary fashion, we must here consider its different fields separately.

Man once "tamed" animals, and he is still capable of this singular achievement. He draws animals into his atmosphere and moves them to accept him, the stranger, in an elemental way, and to respond to him. He wins from them an often astonishing active response to his approach, to his addressing them, and moreover a response which in general is stronger and directer in proportion as his attitude is a genuine saying of *Thou*. Animals, like children, are not seldom able to see through any hypocritical tenderness. But even outside the sphere of taming a similar contact between men and animals sometimes takes place—with men who have in the depths of their being a potential partnership with animals, not predominantly persons of "animal" nature, but rather those whose very nature is spiritual.

An animal is not, like man, twofold: the twofold nature of the primary words *I–Thou* and *I–It* is strange to it, even though it can turn to another being as well as consider objects. Nevertheless we should like to say that there is here a latent twofoldness. That is why we may call this sphere, in respect of our saying of *Thou* out towards the creature, the threshold of mutuality.

It is quite different with those spheres of nature where the spontaneity we share with the animals is lacking. It is part of our concept of a plant that it cannot react to our action towards it: it cannot "respond." Yet this does not mean that here we are given simply no reciprocity at all. The deed or attitude of an individual being is certainly not to be found here, but there is a reciprocity of the being itself, a reciprocity which is nothing but being in its course (*Seiend*). That living wholeness and unity of the tree, which denies itself to the sharpest glance of the mere investigator and discloses itself to the glance of one who says *Thou*, is there when he, the sayer of *Thou*, is there: it is he who vouchsafes to the tree that it manifest this unity and wholeness; and now the tree which is in being manifests them. Our habits of thought make it difficult for us to see that here, awakened by our attitude, something lights up and approaches us from the course of being. In the sphere we are talking of we have to do justice, in complete candour, to the reality which discloses itself to us. I should like to describe this large sphere, stretching from stones to stars, as that of the pre-threshold or preliminal, i.e., the stage before the threshold.

3

Now the question arises concerning the sphere which in the same imagery may be termed the sphere above the threshold, the superliminal, i.e., the sphere of the lintel which is over the door: the sphere of the spirit.

Here too a division must be made between two fields, which goes deeper, however, than the division in nature. It is the division between on the one hand what of spirit has already entered the world and can be perceived in it by means of our senses, and on the other hand what of spirit has not yet entered the world but is ready to do so, and becomes present to us. This division is based on the fact that I can as it were point out to you, my reader, the structure of the spirit which has already entered the world; but I cannot point out the other. I can refer you to the structures of the spirit which are "to hand," in the world that is common to us, no less than a thing or a being of nature, as to something accessible to you in reality or in potentiality. But I cannot refer to that which has not yet entered the world. If I am asked where then the mutuality is to be found here, in this boundary region, then all I can do is indicate indirectly certain events in man's life, which can scarcely be described, which experience spirit as meeting; and in the end, when indirect indication is not enough, there is nothing for me but to appeal, my reader, to the witness of your own mysteries—buried, perhaps, but still attainable.

Let us return, then, to the first realm, that of what is "to hand."
Here we can adduce examples.

Let the questioner make present to himself one of the tradi-
tional sayings of a master who died thousands of years ago; and let
him attempt, as well as he can, to take and receive the saying with
his ears, that is, as though spoken by the speaker in his presence,
even spoken to him. To do this he must turn with his whole being
to the speaker (who is not to hand) of the saying (which is to
hand). This means that he must adopt towards him who is both
dead and living the attitude which I call the saying of *Thou*. If he
succeeds (and of course his will and his effort are not adequate for
this, but he can undertake it again and again), he will hear a voice,
perhaps only indistinctly at first, which is identical with the voice
he hears coming to him from other genuine sayings of the same
master. Now he will no longer be able to do what he could do so
long as he treated the saying as an object—that is, he will not be
able to separate out of the saying any content or rhythm: but he
receives only the indivisible wholeness of something spoken.

But this is still bound to a person, to what a person may have at
any time to say in his words. What I mean is not limited to the con-
tinued influence of any personal life in words. Therefore I must
complete my description with another example to which no personal quality clings. I choose, as always, an example which has
powerful memories for some people: this time the Doric pillar,
wherever it appears to a man who is ready and able to turn to it. Out
of a church wall in Syracuse, in which it had once been immured, it
first came to encounter me: mysterious primal mass represented in
such simple form that there was nothing individual to look at, nothing individual to enjoy. All that could be done was what I did: took
my stand, stood fast, in face of this structure of spirit, this mass penetrated and given body by the mind and hand of man. Does the
concept of mutuality vanish here? It only plunges back into the
dark, or it is transformed into a concrete content which coldly
declines to assume conceptual form, but is bright and reliable.

From this point we may look over into that other realm, the realm of what is "not to hand," of contact with "spiritual being," of the *arising* of word and form.

Spirit become word, spirit become form—in some degree or other everyone who has been touched by the Spirit and did not shut himself to it, knows about the basic fact of the situation—that this does not germinate and grow in man's world without being sown, but arises from this world's meetings with the other. Not meetings with Platonic ideas—of which I have no direct knowledge at all and which I am not in a position to understand as what is in course of being (*Seiendes*); but meetings with the Spirit which blows around us and in us. Again and again I am reminded of the strange confession of Nietzsche when he described the event of "inspiration" as taking but not asking who gives. Even if we do not ask we should "thank."

He who knows the breath of the Spirit trespasses if he desires to get power over the Spirit or to ascertain its nature and qualities. But he is also disloyal when he ascribes the gift to himself.

4

Let us look afresh at what is said here of meetings with what is of nature and what is of spirit, and let us look at them together.

May we then—it may now be asked—speak of "response" or "address," which come from outside everything to which, in our consideration of the orders of being, we adjudge spontaneity and consciousness, as of something that happens in the world of man in which we live, just in this way—as a response or an address? Has what is here described any other validity than that of a "personifying" metaphor? Is there not a danger here of a problematic "mysticism," blurring the boundaries which are drawn, and which must be drawn, by all rational knowledge?

The clear and firm structure of the *I–Thou* relationship, familiar to everyone with a candid heart and the courage to pledge it, has not a mystical nature. From time to time we must come out of our habits of thought in order to understand it; but we do not have to leave the primal norms which determine human thinking about reality. As in the realm of nature, so in the realm of spirit—the spirit which lives on in word and work, and the spirit which wishes to become word and work: what is effected upon us may be understood as something effected by the ongoing course of being (*Seiendes*).

5

In the next question we are no longer concerned with the threshold, the preliminary and the superliminal of mutuality, but with mutuality itself as the door into our existence.

The question is, how is it with the *I-Thou* relationship between men? Is it always entirely reciprocal? Can it always be, may it always be? Is it not—like everything human—delivered up to limitation by our insufficiency, and also placed under limitation by the inner laws of our life together?

The first of these two hindrances is well enough known. From your own glance, day by day, into the eyes which look out in estrangement of your "neighbour" who nevertheless does need you, to the melancholy of holy men who time and again vainly offered the great gift—everything tells you that full mutuality is not inherent in men's life together. It is a grace, for which one must always be ready and which one never gains as an assured possession.

Yet there are some *I-Thou* relationships which in their nature may not unfold to full mutuality if they are to persist in that nature.

Elsewhere[1] I have characterised the relationship of the gen-

---

[1]"Education," section III of Between Man and Man.

uine educator to his pupil as being a relationship of this kind. In order to help the realisation of the best potentialities in the pupil's life, the teacher must really *mean* him as the definite person he is in his potentiality and his actuality; more precisely, he must not know him as a mere sum of qualities, strivings and inhibitions, he must be aware of him as a whole being and affirm him in this wholeness. But he can only do this if he meets him again and again as his partner in a bipolar situation. And in order that his effect upon him may be a unified and significant one he must also live this situation, again and again, in all its moments not merely from his own end but also from that of his partner: he must practise the kind of realisation which I call inclusion) (*Umfassung*).

But however much depends upon his awakening the *I–Thou* relationship in the pupil as well—and however much depends upon the pupil, too, meaning and affirming him as the particular person he is—the special educative relation could not persist if the pupil for his part practised "inclusion," that is, if he lived the teachers' part in the common situation. Whether the *I–Thou* relationship now comes to an end or assumes the quite different character of a friendship, it is plain that the specifically educative relation as such is denied full mutuality.

Another no less illuminating example of the normative limitation of mutuality is presented to us in the relation between a genuine psychotherapist and his patient. If he is satisfied to "analyse" his, i.e., to bring to light unknown factors from his microcosm and to set to some conscious work in life the energies which have been transformed by such an emergency then he may be successful in some repair work. At best he may help a soul which is diffused and poor in structure to collect and order itself to some extent. But the real matter, the regeneration of an atrophied personal centre, will not be achieved. This can only be done by one who grasps the buried latent unity of the suffering soul with the great glance of the doctor: and this can only be attained in the person-to-person attitude of a partner, not by the consideration and examination of an object. In order that he may coherently further the liberation and actualisation of that unity in a new accord of the person with the world, the psychotherapist, like the educator, must stand again and again not merely at his own pole in the bipolar relation, but also with the strength of present realisation at the other pole, and experience the effect of his own action. But again, the specific "healing" relation would come to an end the moment the patient thought of, and succeeded in, practising "inclusion" and experiencing the event from the doctor's pole as well. Healing, like educating, is only possible to the one who lives over against the other, and yet is detached.[1]

The most emphatic example of normative limitation of mutuality could be provided by the pastor with a cure of souls, for in this instance an "inclusion" coming from the other side would attack the sacral authenticity of the commission.

Every *I–Thou* relationship, within a relation which is specified as a purposive working of one part upon the other, persists in virtue of a mutuality which is forbidden to be full.

6

In this context only one question more must be discussed, but it must be discussed since it is incomparably the most important of all.

The question is, how can the eternal *Thou* in the relation be at once exclusive and inclusive? How can the *Thou*–relationship of man to God, which is conditioned by an unconditioned turning

---

[1]Cf. Martin Buber, *Pointing the Way: Collected Essays,* ed. and tr. by Maurice Friedman (New York: Harpers, 1957), "Healing Through Meeting," pp. 93–97. See also Martin Buber, "Guilt and Guilt Feelings," tr. by M. Friedman, *Psychiatry,* ibid.

to him, diverted by nothing, nevertheless include all other *I–Thou* relations of this man, and bring them as it were to God?

Note that the question is not about God, but about our relation to him. And yet in order to be able to answer I must speak of him. For our relation to him is as above contradictions as it is, because he is as above contradictions as he is.

Of course we speak only of what God is in his relation to a man. And even that is only to be expressed in paradox; more precisely, by the paradoxical use of a concept; more precisely still, by the paradoxical combination of a substantive concept with an adjective which contradicts its normal content. The assertion of this contradiction must yield to the insight that the indispensable description of the object by this concept can be justified only in this way. The content of the concept is revolutionised, transformed, and extended—but this is indeed what we experience with every concept which we take out of immanence—compelled by the reality of faith—and use with reference to the working of transcendence.

The description of God as a Person is indispensable for everyone who like myself means by "God" not a principle (although mystics like Eckhart sometimes identify him with "Being") and like myself means by "God" not an idea (although philosophers like Plato at times could hold that he was this): but who rather means by "God," as I do, him who—whatever else he may be—enters into a direct relation with us men in creative, revealing and redeeming acts, and thus makes it possible for us to enter into a direct relation with him. This ground and meaning of our existence constitutes a mutuality, arising again and again, such as can subsist only between persons. The concept of personal being is indeed completely incapable of declaring what God's essential being is, but it is both permitted and necessary to say that God is *also* a Person. If as an exception I wished to translate what is meant by this into philosophical language, that of Spinoza, I should have to say that of God's infinitely many attributes we men do not know two, as Spinoza thinks, but three: to spiritual being (in which is to be found the source of what we call spirit) and to natural being (which presents itself in what is known to us as nature) would be added the attribute of personal being. From this attribute would stem my and all men's being as person, as from those other attributes would stem my and all men's being as spirit and being as nature. And only this third attribute of personal being would be given to us to be known direct in its quality as an attribute.

But now the contradiction appears in the appeal to the familiar content of the concept person. This says that it is indeed the property of a person that its independence should consist in itself, but that it is limited in its total being by the plurality of other independent entities; and this can of course not be true of God. This contradiction is countered by the paradoxical description of God as the absolute Person, i.e., the Person who cannot be limited. It is as the absolute Person that God enters into direct relation with us. The contradiction yields to deeper insight.

As a Person God gives personal life, he makes us as persons become capable of meeting with him and with one another. But no limitation can come upon him as the absolute Person, either from us or from our relations with one another; in fact we can dedicate to him not merely our persons but also our relations to one another. The man who turns to him therefore need not turn away from any other *I–Thou* relation; but he properly brings them to him, and lets them be fulfilled "in the face of God."

One must, however, take care not to understand this conversation with God—the conversation of which I have to speak in this book and in almost all the works which followed—as something happening solely alongside or above the everyday. God's speech to men penetrates what happens in the life of each one of us, and all that happens in the world around us, biographical and historical, and makes it for you and me into instruction, message, demand. Happening upon happening, situation upon situation, are enabled and empowered by the personal speech of God to demand of the human person that he take his stand and make his decision. Often enough we think there is nothing to hear, but long before we have ourselves put wax in our ears.

The existence of mutuality between God and man cannot be proved, just as God's existence cannot be proved. Yet he who dares to speak of it, bears witness, and calls to witness him to whom he speaks—whether that witness is now or in the future.

MARTIN BUBER
Jerusalem, October 1957

Translated by RONALD GREGOR SMITH
Glasgow, November 1957

ABOUT THE AUTHOR

Martin Buber was born in Vienna in 1878, the child of a Jewish family. A prominent Zionist and member of the German Jewish intellectual class wiped out in the Holocaust, he was the editor of a renowned magazine and lectured at the University of Frankfurt from 1924 to 1933. In the first years of Hitler's rule, he stayed in Germany until he had to emigrate in 1938, and from then on he taught at Hebrew University in Jerusalem. In Israel, he became a forthright advocate for efforts to improve understanding between Israelis and Arabs. He died in 1965.